MW01093804

Edgar Cayce's Sacred Stones

Edgar Cayce's Sacred Stones

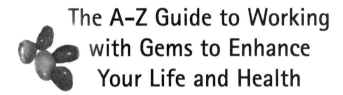

The A–Z Guide to Working
with Gems to Enhance
Your Life and Health

Shelley Kaehr, PhD

A.R.E. Press
Since 1931

A.R.E. Press • Virginia Beach • Virginia

Copyright © 2015
by Shelley Kaehr

7th Printing, February 2021

Printed in the U.S.A.

All rights reserved. No part of this book may be reproduced or transmitted in any form or by any means, electronic or mechanical, including photocopying, recording, or by any information storage and retrieval system, without permission in writing from the publisher.

A.R.E. Press
215 67th Street
Virginia Beach, VA 23451-2061

ISBN 13: 978-0-87604-817-7

Edgar Cayce Readings ©1971, 1993–2007
by the Edgar Cayce Foundation.
All Rights Reserved.

A Note to the Reader

Edgar Cayce's readings are numbered to provide confidentiality. The first set of numbers refers to the individual or group for whom the reading was given. The second set of numbers refers to the number in the series from which the reading was taken. For example, 254-8 identifies the eighth reading that was given to the subject who was assigned #254. It is important to remember that the readings were given for individuals even though they carry a universality of content. With the physical readings, however, it should be noted that the information is not meant to be used for self-diagnosis or self-treatment. Any medical problems need the supervision and advice of a health care professional.

Unless otherwise noted, the King James Bible has been used for biblical quotations.

Cover design by Christine Fulcher

Contents

Part Three

Stones of the Bible **167**

Acknowledgments

This book is the culmination of years of research and study, and I am very happy to be working again with Edgar Cayce's Association for Research and Enlightenment, the A.R.E. I appreciate their help in bringing this project to fruition.

To Edgar Cayce, whose work has inspired my life.

To Dr. Raymond Moody and Auda Marie, who first introduced me to my friends at the A.R.E.

To Cassie McQuagge, Kevin Todeschi, and John Van Auken, I greatly appreciate your vision and support of this project.

To editor extraordinaire, Mary Warren Pinnell, I owe a debt of gratitude for your insight and expertise.

Special thanks to James and Linda Joy and Priscilla Thompson for letting me work with your stones.

Also to my great friends Sandi, Pat, Paula, Sheniqua, Linnea, Brenda, Cindy, and Tammy. And of course, to my family, Mickey, Gail, and Mark.

I thank you all.

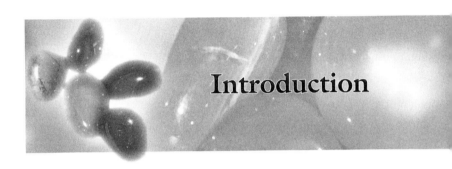

Introduction

It's hard to believe that the first book I wrote for the A.R.E. Press was published ten years ago in 2005. Time flies, as they say.

For the past several years, I had an inner knowing that someday I would write one more book for the A.R.E. The trouble was that I had no idea what it would be.

The moment that my first book about gemstones, minerals, metals, and more was published, I continued with my research and discovered there were many more aspects of this material to explore. After various visions and dreams concerning the fact that I needed to finish something else regarding the Edgar Cayce material, I still had no specific answers about what to write.

For years, I have had an idea floating around me to write a book called *Stones of the Bible*. Initially, I wanted to write that book as an answer to critics who believe that the power of gemstones is evil. The reality is that nothing could be further from the truth. Gemstones have played an important part not only in the Bible but also in many other civilizations.

Little did I know for all these years that these two ideas were similar. Back in 2013, I began a lengthy process of revisiting all of my previously published work. I reread every word, contemplating what I had written and asking myself what I might like to expand upon in the future.

When I read the Cayce material again, I realized that this book more than any of the others had profoundly influenced my thinking and inspired me in many other projects through the years. I soon realized that I was not finished exploring this topic. Although my first book has what I consider to be an abundance of information, I knew that there was much more to explore.

So I find myself once again immersed in the work of the world's greatest psychic. As always, it is my honor to work with the Association for Research and Enlightenment in order to revisit and expand my thoughts from the prior work into this latest compilation. I hope you will enjoy the material.

Life is mysterious. Some circumstances feel like they are "meant to be," and while we may have a knowing of when we would prefer for certain things to happen, sometimes our situations unfold in longer periods of time than what we initially imagine. I believe the time is *now* for this book!

PART

ONE

1 How and Why Gem Healing Works

Before we begin our journey together, we need to discuss how and why gem healing works in the first place.

Everything in the universe consists of vibrations, and this idea is highlighted in much of the Cayce material.

Recently after a long period of working non-stop over the holidays, I developed a headache that lasted for three days. It was so severe that I had no choice but to go to bed and rest. When we need rest but refuse to listen to subtle clues, the body will eventually make the decision for us. Such was the case with my headache.

I live in the Dallas area, and we had experienced a very cold period with little sunshine throughout the month of December. When the sun finally came out, so did the pollen and other unwanted pollutants that blew in from all over the place.

On the sunniest and most beautiful day we'd seen in quite some time, I found myself indoors and in bed with the covers over my head. It was a challenging time for me, to say the least. For the first part of my confinement, aside from trying to hold still so that my head wouldn't hurt, I noticed that my mind was running a mile a minute.

I had been listening to some classical Christmas music in my car, and unfortunately the entire album played over and over in my mind for a day and a half. Once the music ran its course, other thoughts arose and languished about movies I had watched on the Hallmark Channel. Slowly, those faded away.

By the third day, I started thinking about memories from the deep past. By then, with my headache ever present, I escalated the situation from taking baby aspirin to adding sinus pills, which I absolutely hate to do.

Once my headache finally cleared up, my feet and legs began buzzing. Still completely out of whack, I called a friend to tell her that I was sure I was experiencing a true frequency sickness of some kind.

I was so "out of it" the first day that it wasn't until the second day before I finally got up and selected some rocks. I chose my favorite citrine for my solar plexus, some amethyst for my eye sockets, a carnelian for my abdomen, and some quartz for the collarbone and neck area.

Within about twenty minutes of laying the gems on my body, I began to feel better. The stones, along with a vaporizer filled with eucalyptus, a lavender pillow on my eyes, and music consisting of alpha waves, all worked together to help me turn the corner in my healing.

This example of using stones explains how working with gems or any vibrational remedy can be successful. When you feel out of alignment in any way—and normally on a much more subtle level than what I just described—you need something to help you to restore your alignment.

Gems and stones, along with music, essential oils, and other wonderful tools that we have at our disposal, are very beneficial for realigning us with our natural healthy balance.

Gem healing is like music. Have you ever heard people trying to play music when it is out of tune? There is something off, and it doesn't sound quite right. That is what happens to the body—the physical body, as well as the energetic body. On the contrary, when you hear singing or playing that is harmonious, it lifts the spirit as though the heavens have parted.

When a guitar is off tune, the guitarist must strum a note and adjust the strings to bring the whole instrument back into harmony. We are similar. The influences of other people, daily stress, environmental toxins, and more add up until we become out of harmony with our blueprint of perfection, which is how we feel when we are in perfect alignment.

We *can* get back on track. As I recently experienced, sometimes all it takes is slowing down. However, if we don't stop and listen to our bodies long enough to take the proper steps to realign, we might develop some unhealthy discomfort or dis–ease.

I am extremely concerned about the idea of frequency sickness. Our society is often so plugged into phones, computers, televisions, and other devices that we have become out of sync with nature. This is not good!

During those few days when I was ill, I could not stand the sight of any screens or loud sounds. I was literally sick of anything electronic. I had to unplug. I am a very sensitive person, and I am greatly concerned about the masses that may be unaware of what electronics are doing to us. I certainly believe that technology has been a blessing to society in many ways. Communication has become more accessible, but on the other side of the coin, various health issues are arising. As they continue to emerge, I believe we will see more ramifications in the future.

Now more than ever, it is extremely beneficial to understand Cayce's work and to learn how to use natural methods to shift our energy when necessary.

Subtle Bodies

Aside from the physical body, there are three areas of energy within all of us. Actually, there is just one big energy field, but I like to break it down in order to work with it more easily.

The first is the etheric energy layer. This is the field that resides closest to your physical body and is most intricately tied to your health and well–being. If you are blocked here, it will result in an actual, physical illness.

Second is the mental or emotional body, which is six inches away from the body. This is where our memories and emotions are stored. When we do not adequately express our emotions, this area is affected.

Finally, the causal or spiritual body is about a foot away from your physical body and extends to infinity. I believe that all of our challenges in life begin here. Some challenges derive from karma that we incarnated here to work on, and some challenges are new lessons that we have decided to take on after our birth. If we can address our issues at this level, then we do not need to be concerned with the emotional aspects or physical aspects of our energy bodies. That is easier said than done, of course! As my story about being ill demonstrates, we do not normally make changes unless there is mental or physical discomfort first.

When you place a stone on your body, that mineral exists at a higher vibrational frequency than that of the body. Because it is natural and free from the mental or emotional garbage that affects the rest of us, the stone holds its own. When introduced to the physical shell, it will create a change in the above-mentioned energy fields.

Different stones bring different qualities to us. Do you need love, health, or money/security? Depending on what you want to create, certain stones hold a frequency for those circumstances or attributes. By using the stones, your field can begin to shift and align in order for you to attract what you want. We will explore how this energy shift works throughout this book.

Chakras

The other way gems work is to align us with the frequencies of colors in the rainbow spectrum as well as the colorful energy centers of light within each one of us.

Crown chakra:
Color—white
Location—top of the head
The crown center connects you to your higher power. If this area is blocked, you will feel disconnected from life and depressed. Clear crystals are best to help open your crown.

Third Eye chakra:
Color—violet
Location—center of the forehead
The third eye is the seat of your intuition. Amethyst, which we will discuss later in the book, is a carrier of the violet ray and will help to open this center.

Throat chakra:
Color—blue

Location—Under the Adam's apple, just above the collarbone

The throat center helps us to speak our truth. Sapphire is a carrier of the blue ray and will help to open this center. There will be an entire section about sapphire later in this book.

Heart chakra:
Color—green or pink

Location—near your physical heart, in the middle of the chest

Society has many heart issues that are both physical and spiritual. Learning to love others and ourselves is the key for this energy center. You can use rose quartz or emerald to assist in opening the heart. There will be more on emerald, the carrier of the green ray, later in the book.

Solar Plexus chakra:
Color—yellow

Location—stomach, at the convergence of the ribcage

The solar plexus chakra is the seat of your personal power and material abundance, representing courage and manifestation on the physical plane. Citrine is the carrier of the yellow ray. Citrine is amethyst that has been heated up by either natural sunlight or, in many cases, artificial means. A wonderful stone, citrine never needs to be cleansed as most other stones do. It is very good to use for opening up all of the chakra centers, and it will energize you. A delightful by–product of citrine is that it will bring cash and money into your life (there is a difference between "abundance" and money). Known as the "Merchant's Stone," citrine will stimulate growth when you put it in your cash register or wallet.

Sacral chakra:
Color—orange

Location—two inches below the naval

The sacral center is about creativity and productivity in the world at large. Carnelian is a carrier of the orange ray and beneficial to use on this area. More is written about carnelian later in the book.

Root chakra:
Color—red
Location—base of the spine

The root chakra helps connect you to the earth, grounding you in the physical body. Ruby is the carrier of the red ray and is wonderful to use for grounding. A remarkable healer, we will explore ruby at length in a later section.

Healing Self and Others

Once you understand how and why gem healing works, it's time to put that knowledge to use by healing yourself and others with the stones.

Back to the earlier story about my frequency sickness—after I began unplugging my electronics, I felt immeasurably better. Nevertheless, I felt I needed more.

Mercury was about to go retrograde, and I wanted to take a short trip to a cabin where I could be completely away from everything familiar as well as from the electronics.

I packed my bags and left on the first day of the retrograde period, which by the way is a perfect time for realigning and reevaluating things. Besides, electronics often don't work well during these periods, so what better time to get away?

The first day while I was in the cabin, the rain poured nonstop for twenty-four hours. Thick trees surrounded the cabin, and my friend and I were literally trapped inside, forced to be still and quiet.

I had packed all of my favorite stones for our retreat, many of which you will be reading about shortly. Each stone has a particular frequency and when introduced to the body will assist in making the needed changes.

While I was there, I ate only fresh fruits and vegetables to cleanse my system. Most of us believe that our diets are healthy. But even if you eat only organic, gluten-free, and other types of healthful food every single day of your life, the body still needs a break from its familiar routine. Such was the case for me. I decided to change my diet, and by doing so, my energy frequencies were also shifted. That shift, along with using various stones that you will read about in this book, helped me a great deal. The experience proved incredibly healing to my mind, body, and spirit. I felt refreshed by the time I went home after just a few days.

Self-Healing

One thing to keep in mind with self–healing is that while it is normally not considered nice or polite to think of yourself before others, sometimes you have to. If you're run down, how can you hope to be of aid to anyone else?

When I do self–healing, I like to lie on my back and place stones on my heart center, my torso, and my forehead. In addition, I often place a crystal at the top of my head on my pillow to help open the crown. Sometimes the placement varies, depending on what I believe I need at the time.

Please remember that there is no right or wrong in this method. Your intuition will let you know what is best for you. Simply place the stones on or around the body, leaving them there while you take a brief nap or meditation. When you awake, the stones will have assisted you in producing the needed shift, as they did for me.

Healing Others

To heal others, use the same process. I normally work with a massage table. The client is positioned face up to start. Midway through the session, the client faces down, similar to the progression of a massage. I place whatever stones I am guided to use on the body and along the sides of the legs.

Years ago, I was taught to hold a big stone chunk in one hand and wave it over the energy fields of the body. This technique is called an energetic bath, and it is powerful for moving the fields to push out old, unwanted energy while allowing in good, new energy.

Amethyst is my favorite stone to use for the energy bath. Its frequency is higher than most other stones, yet nearly everyone responds to it. I will discuss the energy bath in greater detail in the section on amethyst.

How Long the Session Should Last

If you've been trained in Reiki or other healing modalities, one of the most interesting things to do is to work on people in a group setting. The participants normally start with a brief prayer, and then the healing begins. In the silence, it is interesting to notice how the hands of the practitioners will heat up. The hands will cool off at some point, indicating that the healing is complete.

In a group setting, you will see that usually within seconds of each other, the healers will back away and place their hands into the prayer mode.

Gems are similar. In my own self-healing, after "napping" along with the stones, I will suddenly wake up feeling refreshed. I will know that the energy shift has occurred.

Likewise, when I work on others, sometimes I will feel the energy taper off. In several cases, I have seen some stones literally fall to the ground when they are finished working!

It is truly interesting. I encourage you to experiment for yourself to discover what works best for you.

HOW TO WORK WITH GEMS AND STONES

First, we will discuss how you should work with stones. I discovered a wonderful Cayce reading, which I have split into pieces here because it brings up so many important points about how and why stones work.

Selecting the Right Stone

Q: How will I know when I have found this stone that is most useful for my purposes?
A: When there is found that which is sufficiently clear for the transmission of light and that which may be held in the hand for five to ten minutes and then set aside and listening hear the movements or the vibrations given off from the emanations from self.   440-11

The Cayce readings explain beautifully what I've been trying to tell people for years—that to a certain extent, the stone chooses you and not the other way around. You simply have to listen and pay attention to how you feel, and then you will know which one is right for you.

I love shopping for rocks. It's one of my favorite hobbies. Whenever I am around a bunch of mineral specimens, I am like a kid in a candy store. When I first approach a collection of stones, I reach out to pick one up. When you pick up the first stone to which you are energetically drawn, your soul is talking. On an innate and energetic level, you have connected to that stone for a reason.

And if you're faced with many choices (as I am), you may often put the first stone aside in favor of another that may be more physically attractive. Don't do it!

As the Source says in the above reading, give it some time, pick it up, set aside both the first stone you saw and then the more attractive one, and think about which one is actually speaking to you. Invariably, it will be the first piece you selected.

Trust yourself to make the best selection. If you quiet your mind and access your higher self, the right choice will be clear. You might question yourself. "Is this right? Should I get something else?" If possible, go ahead and take both, but if you must pick only one, choose the one that buzzes in your hand or gives you an especially positive feeling.

What about Physical Properties?

Q: Should it be translucent to light?
A: Should be transparent, or sufficient for the light to pass through.   440-11

I found this part of the reading to be extremely exciting. I've worked with nearly all of the gems in the mineral kingdom over the years because I can't stop myself from buying them! Some of the stones are translucent, and some are not. Different stones will bring different feelings to people. In the above section of this reading, Source discusses a translucent stone because light passes through it, intensifying the healing.

Many stones vibrate to notes on a musical scale or to colors in the rainbow spectrum. When light passes through the gem, the healing properties are indeed better utilized by the body.

Clear crystal is especially receptive to light, which we will discuss later in the book. Crystals are powerful to work with because they can be used alongside any other stone to amplify the energy and speed up the healing.

I recommend using clear quartz crystals with any of the physically denser stones so that the light will pass through your piece and enter the stone you want to work with, amplifying the desired effects. Try this combination and watch your results improve!

In combining crystals with other stones, you will be more likely to feel the energy. Not everybody is sensitive to healing energy. Some of you are visual, some are auditory, and others are touchy–feely types. The fact that you cannot feel a stone working for you does not necessarily mean that it isn't working.

I have perused many readings where Cayce recommended stones for people, and they wrote letters back to him saying they felt more mentally at peace while using the rocks but did not necessarily experience any actual energy from them. That is fine!

Just know and believe that it works. Trust that if you are guided to a stone and actually use it, you will benefit from the energy whether that information is in your conscious awareness or not.

How Do I Use Gemstones?

Q: Should this touch the skin wearing it?
A: To be sure. Usually worn, of course, around the neck or over the body, close to the vibrations from the heart or from the breast itself in its vibrations.   440-11

Again, the Source tells us what I've been advising—that yes, the stone should touch your body. The vibrational frequencies of any stone will affect you more if they contact the skin. Nonetheless, wearing them this way for one reason or another is not always possible.

Many of my clients are men who will not be caught dead wearing necklaces or jewelry, so they often carry around tumbled pocket stones in their hands or pockets. Tumbled stones are great because they can be taken out from time to time and rubbed during the day like worry stones. Whether or not you touch the stones physically, they stay in your energy field and positively influence it. Any time a stone is near you, even if it touches cloth, it affects your energy field. If possible, wear stones against your skin and, as mentioned above, over the heart center so that the vibrational benefits will move throughout the entire body.

What Is the Best Place on the Body to Place or Wear a Stone?

. . . You are used to influence the stone to an effect, either upon those to whom it may be given or to bring for self the ability to aid in its abilities as raising the vibrations for self. Hence would come over this particular portion, or if desired, for the better training of self——held over that portion of the hollow on the left side above what is commonly called the collar bone.

440-11

It is interesting to note that I have spent a lot of time recommending sodalite as a stone to balance the thyroid. The soft area above the collarbone is the ideal place to lay the stone during a healing session on a massage table.

Reading this information from the Source makes me feel more than ever that we can indeed tap into an actual consciousness in the world of gem healing. Gemstones contain wisdom and healing that surpasses our conscious awareness.

Is One Setting Better than Another?

Q: What is the best method of cutting, and what metals should be used in mounting?
A: Use in cutting the ordinary use for the precious or semi-precious stones, in whatever shapes or forms——that are usually the larger in the center and tapering toward the outer edge. Of course, not too large for the use to be worn. The mountings would be white gold or silver . . .

440-11

Consistent with my past research—and this is not an area I've discussed much in other books—I believe the advice that the Source gives here is excellent information. Most of the stone settings for minerals used by people in the metaphysical community are silver. I find this use is due to the cost factor involved with other metals. There is also something to be said for metals themselves and how they affect people. Silver is a feminine intuitive, receptive energy and therefore allows those vibrations to come from the stone into the body.

Yellow gold would do the exact opposite as a masculine, outer energy, and it is understandable that white gold might have more receptive energy than yellow gold.

The Bottom Line

The information in this book will give you different ideas and ways of working with the stones. Using your remarkable wisdom and intuition, only you can decide which stones are right for you. Selecting the right piece for you, honoring your intuition as to which setting attracts you, and knowing how long and when you should use your stone are all conditions that your soul will determine.

In the next section, we will discuss the most valuable stones known to humanity as we delve deeper into the marvelous world of gem healing.

PART

TWO

A Note to the Reader

Edgar Cayce's readings are numbered to provide confidentiality. The first set of numbers refers to the individual or group for whom the reading was given. The second set of numbers refers to the number in the series from which the reading was taken. For example, 254-8 identifies the eighth reading that was given to the subject who was assigned #254. It is important to remember that the readings were given for individuals even though they carry a universality of content. With the physical readings, however, it should be noted that the information is not meant to be used for self-diagnosis or self-treatment. Any medical problems need the supervision and advice of a health care professional.

Unless otherwise noted, the King James Bible has been used for biblical quotations.

2 Sacred Stones

The stones listed in this section have played important roles in history and have endured throughout the ages as some of the most beloved and historically important minerals in the world.

■AGATE■

Agate is a variety of quartz, composed primarily of chalcedony.
Found in: Australia, Brazil, Canada, Germany, India, Iran, Scotland, USA
Named for: The agate is named for the Achates River (now called Dirillo) in Sicily.

• Bible •

> And the third row a . . . an agate . . . Exodus 28:19

> And the third row . . . an agate . . . Exodus 39:12

> Syria was thy merchant by reason of the multitude of the wares of thy making: they occupied in thy fairs with emeralds, purple, and broidered work, and fine linen . . . and agate. Ezekiel 27:16

And I will make thy windows of agates . . . Isaiah 54:12

• Cayce Readings •

Agate was mentioned seven times in seven readings.

> As to the astrological aspects, as we find, these are of the specific
> activity. The omen the body should ever wear on the person is
> a Maltese cross or a stone of the agate . . .   500-1

In another fascinating reading, the subject asked Cayce to describe
a drawing that would be useful:

> In the center put (and this should roll from the right side of the
> drawing) the twisted cornucopia, and out of same would come
> rolling the seven virtues—hence seven stones, in the varied
> colors; from agate . . . indicating meekness . . .   533-20

> Hence we find the agate . . . should be *stones* with the vibrations
> and under the influence that the entity may find carrying an
> incense to the finer self that makes for . . . an opening of the
> inner self for the *receptiveness* . . .   707-1

> As to stones, those of the blue, as well as the agate should be
> about.   1397-1

> . . . the agate should be as an amulet, either about the neck or as
> a ring, or worn upon the person.   1401-1

More on Agate

Agates exist worldwide in many shapes sizes and colors, and are extremely healing to the body. Both their color and the part of the world from
which they originate will affect the healing properties.

One of my favorite varieties is the blue lace agate from Botswana, Africa,
which is an exceptional stone to use for communication. Crazy lace agate
from Utah occurs in browns and reds and is used to calm the stomach.
Agates from this area can assist with your spiritual journeys and meditation
and may also help to tap into prior lives that took place in the Wild West.

Another one of my favorite agate stones, which I still have to this day, is a variety from Utah. I call it my UFO agate because the design in the center looks like a flying saucer from the sixties. This agate has sentimental qualities for me because I received it from a dear friend before his death. Stones can bring energy to you by becoming energetic reminders of loved ones or special times in your life.

I think associations with material possessions are interesting. Those items that mean the most to us remind us of a person, time, or place. Holding any such object serves as a time machine, taking us into the past and offering us a sense of nostalgia.

In addition to the fact that an agate brings the user a peaceful sense of being in the world, this stone is nice to have as an anchor to pleasant memories.

I've often said that stones find us for a reason—just as friends do—and I believe that this agate from Utah will likely be with me for my lifetime.

Blue Agate

Stones can serve as reminders of lost loved ones or friends. Several years ago, I discovered an excellent variety of blue agate from Oregon, which turned out to be an outstanding stone to use for grief recovery. Once I started working with it, I loved it so much that I featured it as a selection in my "Rock of the Month Club."

I sent pieces of blue agate to a number of my students and asked them for feedback on what they believed it did for them. Incredibly, their comments were similar to each other and reflected what I already believed about the stone's ability to bring profound feelings of peace and healing to the user. One student used the stone with meditation and felt a reassuring sense of calm. Another student used the blue agate in the evenings and reported greater ease in falling asleep as well as a sense of relaxation in the morning. A third student held the stone while watching TV and reported feeling at peace about some trouble at work. All of them liked the stone and its energetic properties.

Stones have energetic properties based on their type as well as their geological place of origin. Blue represents the throat chakra, which relates to how we communicate in the world, yet the color blue is connected with emotional healing. Any emotions expressed verbally originate in the throat center. We often stuff deep inside of ourselves many emotions or thoughts that we want to express—perhaps for the protection of someone's feelings or for fear of potential negative repercussions. Once a thought occurs in the mind, whether it is physically verbalized or not, it affects the throat center. We will explore this idea further in the sapphire section of this book. Botswana blue lace agate is more of a communication stone, while the Oregon variety of agate aids with emotional healing.

After suffering the loss of my dear cat companion several years ago, I learned firsthand about the fantastic healing energies of this stone. While going through her things, cleaning, and rearranging, I was immediately drawn to my favorite piece of blue agate. The stone seemed to lift the heavy weight of grief from my shoulders at that time, and it also left me feeling more peaceful and serene.

I am convinced that the agate helped me to speed up the necessary processing of the many stages of grief, allowing me to experience and work through all of my emotions with grace and ease.

Unfortunately, all of us will suffer loss in our lifetimes. Whether we lose family members, friends, jobs, or living places, each loss will be challenging for various reasons. Agate will aid the healing process regarding whatever kind of grief might affect us, and for that reason, I highly recommend blue agate as a necessary tool to keep in the medicine bag.

■ ALABASTER ■

Found in: England, France, Germany, Iran, Italy, Pakistan, Spain, USA

Named for: Alabaster is derived from the Greek word, *alabastros*, which was used to define a variety of massive, fine-grained gypsum.

• Bible •

> There came unto him a woman having an alabaster box of very precious ointment, and poured it on his head, as he sat at meat. Matthew 26: 7

> And being in Bethany in the house of Simon the leper, as he sat at meat, there came a woman having an alabaster box of oint-

ment of spikenard very precious; and she brake the box, and
poured it on his head. Mark 14:3

And, behold, a woman in the city, which was a sinner, when she
knew that Jesus sat at meat in the Pharisee's house, brought an
alabaster box of ointment, Luke 7:37

• Cayce Readings •

Alabaster is mentioned three times in three readings. The first mention is in a booklet that was published in April of 1930 by The Association of National Investigators, Inc.:

> And now began preparations for the coming of the great King
> from far away, and for the wedding, and about the castle . . . and
> they erected an entrance of alabaster . . .   254-107, Report #1

While giving a reading to a client, Cayce dreamed about alabaster,
as he noted in the first report:

> I was conscious of the fact of separating my physical self from
> my soul self, my physical self being encased in a box like an ala-
> baster . . . box, from a material I could not describe. It seemed
> the material manifestation of my physical and mental self was
> in the box. I gave the box to someone and felt, as I gave it, 'This
> is one I can trust.' . . .   257-130, Report #1

In another reading, the subject was a high priestess in Egypt and
the term alabaster seemed synonymous with a higher spiritual state
of purity:

> Throughout that particular period we find that the entity
> sojourned in that city where the Temple of Sacrifice and the
> Temple Beautiful performed their functions, their offices, as
> the aid to the people . . . For, few of those had arisen to that
> state in which there were the preparations so as to produce the
> alabaster, or all white, or all relationships that brought or made
> for individuality and better expression for the personality of

the entity throughout that sojourn.   2329-3

More on Alabaster

Alabaster is a vague mineralogical term referring to either gypsum or calcite. Snowy white and often translucent, light can pass through it.

Depending on which variety of alabaster you choose, this material will connect you with the energy of Egypt or ancient Europe—and with any past-life connections you have had in those places. An important material in the ancient world, alabaster assists with tapping into the lifetimes of ancient civilizations by helping to recover skills and memories associated with places such as Egypt, Greece, or Italy.

Ancient Egyptian alabaster is a form of the calcite variety. In the Egyptian reading, Cayce would have referred to calcite alabaster.

Ancient Egyptians used alabaster for sacred objects such as sarcophaguses and other ritual items. King Tutankhamun's tomb was filled with items carved from alabaster.

Oriental alabaster, another term for this stone, refers to the calcite-based marble, which will be discussed in a later section.

One of my most profound adventures was a trip to Egypt back in the year 2000. While in the magnificent city of Luxor, I went to a shop where several people were carving scarab beetles, bowls, and other items from huge blocks of alabaster. It looked like extremely challenging work, but luckily both kinds of alabaster are soft and easy to carve.

The scarab was a sacred symbol of the morning sun and renewal in ancient Egypt. The dung beetle laid eggs in a dung ball and rolled it across the ground, an action that soon became symbolic of the physical embodiment of the creation god Khepri, who moved the morning sun across the sky. Even today, the beetle is considered lucky in Egypt, and these scarabs are considered popular tourist items.

In terms of Biblical probability, the alabaster of the Bible would also be calcite because of its prevalence in the Middle East.

Spiritually speaking, calcite is a wonderful material to use for meditation because it calms the nerves and brings peace to the core or stomach area, connecting you with Mother Earth.

The second type of alabaster is from the material gypsum. Medieval Europeans used this variety of alabaster.

While both materials are soft, the gypsum is even more fragile than the calcite. I am a big fan of the gypsum-based material called selenite, one of the most profound healing stones ever.

Most healing stones require occasional energetic clearing because they take on unwanted energy to help with healing. For that reason, they must be cleansed from time to time. Gypsum materials such as selenite and alabaster are different from most other minerals because they never need cleaning. They do not become bogged down energetically after being used. Alabaster and selenite are of such high frequency that the issues and circumstances of mundane worldly life do not affect them.

Selenite works wonders on the chakra centers and energy fields around the body. Since selenite is often flat, you can use it to clean other stones by placing them on top of it. How long you leave the stone there depends on you. I recommend cleansing for at least twenty minutes. The high-vibrational energy quickly balances unwanted frequencies and cleanses your other stones so that they are ready to use once again. Whether placing the selenite on the body or using it to clean your healing tools, this material creates a higher overall vibration by transforming lower frequencies into pure white light.

I can certainly see how either variety of alabaster might have played a critical role in our spiritual history. Many of the sacred rituals performed in Egypt where priests and priestesses were busy transcending normal reality to access higher realms involved the use of alabaster. Many of us, like the woman who went to Cayce for her reading, have probably lived previous lives in Egypt and performed similar rituals. For that reason, we would all benefit from working with alabaster.

▪ A M E T H Y S T ▪

Found in: Brazil, Burma, Canada, India, Mexico, Namibia, Russia, Sri Lanka, Uruguay, USA

Named for: Amethyst is derived from an Ancient Greek word meaning "not intoxicated" since it was believed to prevent inebriation.

Birthstone: February

• Bible •

> And the third row . . . an amethyst. Exodus 28:19
>
> And the third row . . . an amethyst. Exodus 39:12
>
> . . . the twelfth, an amethyst. Revelation 21:20

• Cayce Readings •

Amethyst is mentioned sixteen times in thirteen documents.

> Well that the entity have the stones or minerals about self when in periods of meditation, or in those periods when it may find itself the more easily attuned to the influences that may use the body, either in the healing forces that flow through—through its attunements, or through the visions and associations of the entity . . . the amethyst. For the color purple should be close to the body, and the perfumes or odors as of lavender have their influence—not in great quantity, but that which makes for attunements.   688-2

> As to the stones . . . amethyst should be a part of that which would be about the entity—because of the very natural vibrations for the entity. For they will bring as an attunement the quieting, and the entity will find that whenever there is a feeling of physical depression, physical reactions that are as dis-ease in the body, the colors in any of these natures or forms will bring quietness to the body; as in having about the body . . . the amethyst color, in cloth, in drapery, in hangings.   1626-1

> In the temple were to be found enormous semi-circular columns . . . inlaid with amethyst . . . 364-13, Report #3

> . . . there were those mines of the precious stones . . . amethyst . . . that came from the sea near what is now called Madagascar . . .   294-148

> . . . In this temple, we find . . . amethyst . . .   364-12

> . . . The omen the body should ever wear on the person is . . . amethyst—for their vibrations are better. But as the body should comprehend in regard to all such influences, it is as to what the

body does about same, not that it relies upon such but knowing
that such influences aid in increasing the ability or efficiency in
the periods of exertion or activity . . .   500-1

The reading mentioned earlier describing the virtues goes on to list
amethyst as one of the desired stones, and Cayce explains why:

. . . the seven virtues—hence seven stones, in the varied colors
. . . the amethyst . . . patience . . .   533-20

Amethyst stones should ever be a portion about the body, either
in amulets or adornments about the body. These in their very vibration will make for an influence that has to do with the entity
in its innate and manifested expressions in its associations.
1035-1

Stones,—the entity should have the amethyst (the white) about
self often. These vibrations will bring greater harmony, in not
only body but in the mental attributes.   1986-1

 In the choice of stones, do wear the amethyst as a pendant
about the neck, as a part of the jewelry. This will also work with
the colors to control temperament.   3806-1

More on Amethyst

Amethysts have long been associated with imparting patience and
allowing people to release addictions with grace and ease. How could
Cayce have consciously known this? This reading demonstrates the
power of the information from the Source. We can attain true wisdom
from Spirit and our ancestors concerning the benefits that various
stones and minerals provide for us.
The Source mentions lavender in one of the readings. Amethyst is
the color of the violet ray, which opens the third eye. If we could assign
an essential oil to that same frequency, it would be lavender because
it aligns with this energy and brings calm and peace to the user. The
Source also mentioned amethyst's ability to calm and quiet the body. By
helping to eliminate what is not needed by a person, amethyst brings a
sense of calm and peace to the energy body, allowing users to become

stable and at one with themselves and their environment.

Amethyst Chunk Energy Bath

In my book *Gemstone Journeys* I discussed how I first discovered the healing properties of gemstones after meeting a shaman who taught me how to use stones to heal the body. He described how to give oneself or others an energetic bath by running rocks through the energy fields surrounding the body. By using your imagination, you envision the energy beginning to move the way you want it to.

Amethyst chunks are best used for the energy bath. Why? Amethyst has a higher frequency than many other stones, making it the best one to get things moving again.

Pets

I have spent a considerable amount of time working with pets. I have found that one stone above all others works well for them, and that is the amethyst. For the same reasons that an amethyst energy bath works on people, I believe that the energy of amethyst assists our pets in moving unwanted energy from their delicate fields in order to restore their natural balance.

I believe that pets are earth angels. They are innocents and as such they perform a great service to mankind by helping us transcend our suffering. Pets are willing to take on our "stuff" to help us shift and rise above any unwanted energy.

When our pets are ill, we owe it to our beloved friends to try to help them. Some stones would be toxic to use on your pet, so I always choose the quartz family—amethyst, rose, or clear quartz. You can place the stones in direct contact with your pet. I have even put stones in a horse's stall to calm the horse down. I arranged for my ill cat to sleep on amethyst chunks until he felt better, and I used clear quartz with an unhappy dog that was in a kennel waiting for his owners to return. Use your imagination; it works! Your intuition will tell you what stone is best to use. While naturally gifted in this area, pets do need a little extra help when they are upset or sick. Gemstones can assist with these energy shifts.

Why This Works So Well

Amethyst is the carrier of the violet ray. As such it can assist the body to move lower frequency energy, while at the same time being energetically accessible to everyone.

By accessible, I mean that some stones have such high vibrations that they are beyond the perception of most people. Some individuals have a difficult time with certain stones energetically. And various minerals may have such a high frequency that some people may not even notice the vibrations at all.

For example, I used to own a beautiful harp. I wanted to play in public, so I called a local bookstore and went there to play. This harp was not the norm. It was an Angel Harp, expressly prepared to play very high-frequency, healing sounds. As I played, I quickly noticed something. Nobody could hear me! Even people who were only a few feet away never bothered to look at the harp or react to the sounds in any way whatsoever.

Quite some time passed, and there I was, playing the harp for the few friends who were with me at the bookstore. I was about to give up when a woman and her daughter walked over, and we had a pleasant chat. Eventually, a few others joined in, but most people in the store had no idea that we were even there. It was like wearing a cloak of invisibility. What I discovered is that unless the people vibrated at a particular frequency, they could not receive the healing from the music. The two frequencies were utterly incompatible.

Stones are the same way! Some stones emit such high vibrations that people cannot notice them. Such stones work in particular instances, but for a mineral to be efficient and shift the vast collective consciousness frequency, it must normally be able to be perceived by most people.

Amethyst is noticeable to everyone and most people respond to it. I've seen this reaction for years at gem shows and shops. Whether or not people are of the mindset to understand consciously how stones can heal, most people react positively to amethyst. Such responses might include commenting on the beauty of the stone. That is enough to prove that someone is getting something from the stone. Amethyst has a high enough frequency, or as Cayce would say—vibration—that things will shift for the better for the person who sees or uses it.

Additionally, because amethyst opens the third eye center, there is no better stone for developing psychic abilities and becoming open to receiving information from other realms.

There is a Greek legend about a girl named Amethyst who travels to pay homage to the goddess Diana. On her way, she encounters Bacchus, the god of wine and libation, who accidentally strikes the girl down and turns her into a white stone. When Diana chastises him, he cries his purple wine-colored tears and turns her into the gorgeous stone that we know today. Ever since then, amethyst (meaning not drunken in Greek) has assisted those who suffer from addictions.

Amethysts help to quell our unhealthy thirst and bring us back into balance. Let's face it—we all are hooked on something, even if it is good for us. Remember the old saying about too much of a good thing? It's hard to admit at times, but addiction is often a part of the human experience.

As a hypnotherapist, I use amethyst stones quite often in sessions. Having the person hold an amethyst chunk can be restorative. Even though it is not being washed over the energy fields, it still causes a shift to occur.

Relationship issues are challenging for many people, and sometimes people become stuck in a bad situation because they cannot find a way out. Amethyst energy assists people who travel into past lifetimes to reveal the source events of painful relationships. The energy of amethysts can help people to see the higher vision and lessons of the past while gently releasing the karmic link in the current incarnation.

So if you find you need to release anything that is no longer serving you, amethysts will help a great deal.

∎ B E R Y L ∎

Found in: Brazil, Columbia, Egypt, Europe, South Africa, USA, Zimbabwe

Named for: The Greek word *beryllos* refers to "blue-green stones of the sea."

Birthstone: March (Aquamarine is a variety of beryl.)

• Bible •

And the fourth row a beryl . . . Exodus 28:20

And the fourth row a beryl . . . Exodus 39:13

His hands are as gold rings set with the beryl . . . Song of Solomon 5:14

The appearance of the wheels and their work was like unto the colour of a beryl . . . Ezekiel 1:16

And when I looked, behold the four wheels by the cherubims, one wheel by one cherub, and another wheel by another cherub: and the appearance of the wheels was as the colour of a beryl stone. Ezekiel 10:9

Thou hast been in Eden the garden of God; every precious stone was thy covering . . . the beryl . . . Ezekiel 28:13

His body also was like the beryl . . . Daniel 10:6

. . . the eighth, beryl . . . Revelation 21:20

• Cayce Readings •

Beryl was mentioned fourteen times in twelve documents.

Q: Can you give the exact location where sufficient Beryl deposits can be found for the most economical and commercial production?
A: Well, this would require a great deal of seeking out . . . .those in the Ural range, and in the Siberian country, show greater quantities . . . in the southern Andes Range or near that border line between the Chilean and the Peruvian . . . In those points, then, where the least *change* has taken place will be found the greater deposits of these beryl.   1734-1

Hence we find . . . the beryl, should be *stones* with the vibrations and under the influence that the entity may find carrying an incense to the finer self that makes for an awakening, an opening of the inner self for the *receptiveness* . . .   707-1

In one reading, Cayce described how Spirit affected material reality:

> ... the ceilings are beryl, the doors are beryl ...   5756-12

> In the temple were to be found enormous semi-circular columns of ... beryl ...   364-13, Report #3

> ... Wear, ever, a beryl, or scarab which would make for safety in the entity's present experience.   1719-1, Report #1

> ... Also in the land now known as Abyssinia ... there were those mines of the precious stones ... beryl ...   294-148

> ... and inlaid with beryl ...   364-12

> ... there were uprisings in the land now known as the Egyptian ... the entity's activities, in the tomb or the small granary, or obelisks yet to be uncovered in the small or first pyramids of beryl.   539-2

> ... the beryl—if it is kept about the body would be well. 568-1

> ... beryl ... and all those things that made for adornment ...
>   1493-1

> ... the beryl ... should be a portion of the entity's dress, *ever*, either worn as an amulet, the ring, or such, will make for a safety in the entity's present experience.   1719-1

More on Beryl

Emerald is the most widely known variety of beryl. Because of its significance throughout history, we will discuss it in an upcoming section of the book.

Pure beryl is actually colorless, but various impurities give this gem a variety of colors. Other beryl varieties are significant and interesting also. We'll explore some of these briefly.

Aquamarine

The name of this gorgeous pale blue variety of beryl comes from the Latin words *aqua* and *marinus*, which mean "water of the sea."

Legend says aquamarines belonged to the treasure chests of mer–

maids. Sailors believed aquamarines would protect them from ship-wrecks and even went so far as to carve statuettes of Neptune and Poseidon from aquamarine stones.

The aquamarine has been a favorite of psychics and intuitives, assisting them in hearing messages from other realms and effectively communicating the information to clients. The blue color ties into the water element, as mentioned earlier with the blue agate. Aquamarine cleanses the emotional body and assists in releasing and expressing emotions.

For those drawn to the sea, aquamarines will help you tap into past lives at sea. Once you recall those experiences, either you will heal from phobias of the water or gain a remembrance of activities and skills acquired during those aquatic lifetimes that will benefit your current incarnation.

Heliodor

Named for the Greek words *helios* and *doron*, which mean "gift from the sun," this greenish-yellow variety of beryl will connect you with solar energies. Heliodor strengthens the solar plexus chakra, making abundance, wealth, and power available to you.

Sometimes confused with golden beryl, the heliodor refers to the greenish-yellow variety, while the pure golden beryl has a yellower color. The healing green hues support you to open your heart and stand in your power.

If you need to garner strength or courage for any endeavor or project, heliodor is an excellent stone to use. Primarily found in Namibia, this stone also occurs in Brazil. The yellow color comes from iron, which is a grounding metal. Grounding is one of the reasons why the greenish-yellow beryl will strengthen your resolve to follow your heart and complete your projects in a timely manner.

Lucid Beryl

White lucid beryl, a colorless variety, does exactly what the name implies by assisting with lucid dreaming and tapping into the wellspring of information available in the unified field during sleep.

Morganite

Pink beryl, named after the famous banker J. P. Morgan, will connect you to the faerie realm and help you communicate with unseen helpers from that world. The pink color comes from the element manganese, a trace mineral.

Epsom salts, or magnesium sulfate, is comprised of the essential element magnesium, which is often confused with manganese. I have long believed magnesium to be essential to healing. Epsom salts cleanses unwanted or negative energy from your field and leaves you feeling refreshed.

Similarly, morganite lifts your energy above normal reality, giving you higher vision. Morganite also removes unwanted vibrations and attunes your inner hearing to higher realms.

Red Beryl

Extremely rare, red beryl from Utah and New Mexico gets its red color from manganese. A powerful energy for opening up to intuitive information, the red beryl will help you to connect with the spirit energies of the desert. Red beryl will also connect you to past lives lived as a Native American. If you have not yet experienced Native American powers in other incarnations, this beryl will allow you to connect with the wisdom of the elders in order to use that knowledge in your current life.

■ BLOODSTONE ■

Heliotrope, a.k.a. bloodstone, is the mineral and is a form of chalcedony.

Found in: Australia, Brazil, Canada, China, India, Scotland, USA

Named for: Heliotrope is derived from Greek words meaning "to turn toward the sun."

Birthstone: Bloodstone is the traditional birthstone for March.

• Bible •

Bloodstone is not mentioned in any versions of the Bible.

• Cayce Readings •

Bloodstone is mentioned sixteen times in fourteen documents.

The A.R.E. asked for feedback about the effects of individual stones and received the following information regarding bloodstone:

> . . . She has worn a bloodstone but at the moment the ring has to be repaired so it has not been worn for some time. While she did wear the bloodstone she noticed no particular effect. Was not aware of any vibrations.   1770-2, Report #14

The Source suggested that bloodstone would bring joy to one client:

> . . . might the entity bring a great deal of joy . . . bloodstone . . .
>   5294-1

The Source also referred to the amazing healing powers of bloodstone in several readings:

> . . . bloodstone to send out most healing vibrations for her body
> . . .   275-11, Report #16

> Q: What precious stone sends out the most healing vibrations for my body?
> A: . . . the bloodstone.   275-31

> Q: What are the entity's stone, mineral and metal?
> A: . . . and as the stone would be the bloodstone . . .   282-7

> Hence the bloodstone . . . should be as a stone that would be about the body . . .   816-3

> . . . the bloodstone, which is—with its vibrations—that element which from the etheronic energies of nature in itself creates the proper environs for vibratory forces about the entity.   824-1

> *Do not* lay aside the rosary! Have about the entity stones that are red; as the bloodstone . . .   1616-1

> Hence the bloodstone . . . is well to ever be about the entity,

upon its body; so that the very vibratory forces of same give—with that of thought in constructive force—creative environs or vibrations for the entity in its use or application.   1770-2

. . . Hence we would wear especially the bloodstone, cut in the form of a triangle, though ovaled on its edges. This about the body brings that vibration which will be beneficial; not merely as a good luck charm, not merely as something upon which to depend, but as an influence, a vibration about the entity.

2163-1

Keep the bloodstone close to the body . . .   2282-1

Q: In what part of the country will entity meet her second husband, and how will she recognize him?
A: . . . He will wear a bloodstone on the third finger of the left hand . . .   2708-2

. . . the others have their varying vibrations as the blood-stone or the others, as the entity has indicated in the things set down during those periods of activity in Egypt as Ark-uen.   3657-1

. . . There are those to whom the bloodstone brings harmony, and less of the tendencies for anger; and so with each. 5294-1

More on Bloodstone

Bloodstone is a term used to describe the dark green variety of chalcedony with red spots. Europeans often refer to this stone as heliotrope, meaning sun turner. The heliotrope name came from the fact that people once believed the stone could turn the rays of the sun red and if placed in water, show the sun as a blood red image.

Chlorite gives bloodstone its dark green color. Iron ore (more commonly known as hematite) causes the red specks to occur.

Although the Bible does not mention bloodstone, legend says that bloodstone was present at the crucifixion of Jesus and that Christ's blood caused the stone's red spots. Just as Christ made his sacrifice on the cross, bloodstone allows people to take on its physical properties to heal. When someone holds a bloodstone, the red color is absorbed into the physical body and disappears. Many believe this healing property is yet another example of how Christ allows us to use his energy to transcend.

I've seen this happen with my own eyes on more occasions than I can count. Both the red flecks and green chlorite disappeared from these stones after people used them for everything from cancers to blood disorders to heart problems. You name it; bloodstone can heal.

I first saw this phenomenon while working with a very ill client who came to see me for hypnosis. He had a chronic lung condition and kept the bloodstones in his pocket for less than twenty-four hours when the green and red stones faded. One of them turned clear. Later, I told people about this occurrence and heard from people from all over the United States and abroad who wrote to report the fact that their stones had turned colors or had become completely clear.

On a number of occasions I sent bloodstones to people with leukemia, muscular dystrophy, or bone cancer. All of them reported some alleviation of symptoms, although as with all healing, sometimes this experience does not mean that the people survive. None of us will make it out of this life alive. We know that. In my opinion, if any vibrational remedy can alleviate pain and suffering—whether physical or emotional—then it is beneficial.

To this day, I am still not sure why bloodstones react this way or which specific ailments they have helped. Our souls are complicated. We come here to learn lessons, many of which are brought to us through illness. I believe stones can assist with the body, mind, and spirit, making it difficult to pinpoint precisely which aspect of a person has received some healing. In the case of the man with the lung condition, I saw him a year later, and he felt better than ever. Whatever healing crisis he had experienced previously had passed.

Bloodstone allows us to see these shifts physically, which contributes to the many reasons it works so well. All the minerals work to affect our energy systems, yet change is hard to believe without seeing it with our own two eyes. Trust is the foundation of faith, and we should be able to trust without requiring physical evidence. However, seeing something with your own eyes strengthens your belief, and that strength carries over into many areas of life. Once someone has that aha moment of seeing the work that bloodstones can achieve, he or she can suspend disbelief in a number of other therapies and benefit from knowing that there is great power in vibrational remedies.

There is only one other stone I've ever seen fade in color from use, and that is the carnelian, which we will discuss in the next section.

The idea of bloodstone's connection to Christ originated during medieval times when people believed its special powers could stop a hemorrhage once the victim touched the stone.

Even in the Cayce readings, we find references to this concept. During one reading, the Source mentions a rosary, which for me further substantiates the connection between the spiritual Christ Consciousness and the bloodstone.

Additionally, people often used bloodstones for carving images of the crucifixion.

Ancient Greeks and Romans believed bloodstone helped strengthen athletes. In my opinion, the bloodstone is the most important of the healing stones for its ability to heal the physical body. The green color from chlorite is a powerful element for healing lungs and other respiratory conditions. Bloodstone can also assist with conditions having to do with blood such as leukemia, blood pressure, or strengthening the veins carrying blood through the body. When in doubt, if there is one stone you should have with you at all times, it is the bloodstone.

■CARNELIAN■
Carnelian is also called the sardine stone since it is similar to sard, or sardius, which is a little harder and darker.

Found in: Brazil, Germany, India, Madagascar, Namibia, Siberia, Uruguay, USA

Named for: Carnelian, which used to be called cornelian, gets its name from the Latin word *carneus* meaning "of the flesh" or from the Cornel cherry, due to its color. Sardius is derived from the Latin word *sarda* meaning "Sardinian" and the Greek word *sardios*, which referred to the ancient capital of the city Lydia in what is now Turkey (formerly Asia Minor).

• Bible •

Carnelian is mentioned in the newer versions of the Bible.

> Then mount four rows of precious stones on it. The first row shall be carnelian . . . Exodus 28:17 (New International Version)

> Then they mounted four rows of precious stones on it. The first
> row was carnelian . . . Exodus 39:10 (NIV)

> You were in Eden, the garden of God; every precious stone
> adorned you: carnelian . . . Your settings and mountings were
> made of gold; on the day you were created they were prepared.
> Ezekiel 28:13 (NIV)

Sardius, which is a name for carnelian from antiquity, appears in
Exodus and also in Ezekiel in the King James Version in the same place
as carnelian is positioned in the breastplate of the high priest:

> And thou shalt set in it settings of stones, even four rows of
> stones: the first row shall be a sardius . . . this shall be the first
> row. Exodus 28:17 (KJV)

> And they set in it four rows of stones: the first row was a sardius
> . . . this was the first row. Exodus 39:10 (KJV)

> Thou hast been in Eden the garden of God; every precious stone
> was thy covering, the sardius . . . the workmanship of thy tablets
> and of thy pipes was prepared in thee in the day that thou wast
> created. Ezekiel 28:13 (KJV)

> . . . the sixth, sardius . . . Revelation 21:20 (KJV)

The Bible also mentions the sardine stone, which was another name
that was used for carnelian:

> And he that sat was to look upon like . . . a sardine stone: and
> there was a rainbow round about the throne. Revelation 4:3
> (KJV)

• Cayce Readings •

Carnelian is not found in the readings, but sardius is mentioned in
one document.

> . . . the stones the entity should have about same, is the sar-
> dius—for this gives for an influence as may be best made in the

entity's influence to understand those laws as apply to man's relationships to the higher forces.   1714-1

More on Carnelian

The oldest named form of silicon dioxide other than quartz, sardius—or carnelian—is an ancient stone that was referred to as sardon (from the Sardon Mountains) in the Middle Ages. Sard is similar to agate without banding, while carnelian, also called red-banded agate, is an orange stone with white bands.

Orange Ray

Color has a profound influence on people, and gems are an excellent way to work with color in your life.

Several years ago, I started experimenting with color by painting the walls in my office outrageous colors, including bright orange and taxicab yellow. After several months, I finally settled on a bright purple.

I happen to love the color purple because it resonates with the third eye and brings an ethereal feeling of relaxation to any space. The trouble with having purple walls was that I wasn't getting any work accomplished! I was so relaxed that for a long time, I was not consciously aware of what was happening.

The first "clue" I had that something was off was when I bought myself a bag of carnelian stones. I have always loved carnelian and have used it successfully to stimulate creativity.

I put the stones in a container and placed them on my desk. I immediately noticed an increase in energy, which translated into several projects finally becoming completed.

Carnelian vibrates at the frequency of the orange ray, opening up the sacral chakra and stimulating creativity.

Creativity comes in many forms. You may not be an artist, singer, or writer, but you may have the energy for creating projects in business. You may be an inventor of some amazing new technology or an innovator whose brilliant ideas can transform an old industry into something for the twenty-first century. You may have a gift for working with people and bringing them together for a common cause. Whatever your talent and whatever makes your heart sing, carnelian will open up the necessary energetic channels, making life force available so that you will achieve completion on any project or higher calling.

Once I became fully aware of the fact that my purple walls were causing me to lollygag around, I changed the color and transformed myself back into a productive state. I owe that positive change to the marvelous carnelian stone!

Sard in Ancient Times

Sard is an ancient stone that has been used for eons by many different cultures and civilizations. Persian carnelian adorned the Taj Mahal, and Roman soldiers believed the stone gave them courage in battle. Even the people in ancient times could sense the creative energy of sard.

Allergy Relief

I discovered by accident another surprising use for the carnelian stone. Carnelian can help with allergies. Several years ago, a friend of mine said she felt the carnelian stone clear out her sinuses, so I tried it and found it helped me, also. Since then, I have told people about this attribute and have found that many of my students concur with the benefit.

Fading with Use

In the previous chapter, I mentioned that like the bloodstone, carnelian is the only other stone in the mineral kingdom that I have personally seen fade in color after using it for healing. I have experienced this occurrence firsthand with several different pieces of carnelian over the years. Whereas the bloodstones have successfully assisted several people I've worked with, the fading carnelian seems more like a personal phenomenon for me. An example of this experience would be like taking the Cayce advice from the readings, knowing that it had helped one person. I believe I have a spiritual connection to carnelian, needing the energy from the stone for some vibrational reason, which causes it to fade for me.

When I described the changing color of bloodstones earlier, I should explain that the fading has never happened when I have personally worked with those stones. My energy has never caused a bloodstone to fade from its green color.

Using carnelian is another story for me. Perhaps my writing causes me to absorb the energy from these stones. When meditating with carnelians, I've noticed that when I use them overnight and sleep with them in the bed, they are often paler in the morning than when I started. Somehow they are allowing me to use them for a boost in energy, for which I am eternally grateful.

So far, I have not received reports about this phenomenon from other people because it is not something I have discussed until now. If you work with carnelian and find that it is fading on you, bless the stone for allowing you to use its energy, and then feel free to let me know by email! I am sure other people might have had the same experience. I believe that I use the stone for creativity, but other people might use carnelian for other situations or qualities.

Someone suffering from bad allergies who uses carnelian might fade the color. I am not sure of that fact, but it would make sense. I have never suffered from bad allergies other than right at the beginning of springtime when the flowers bloom. If you're like many people who have a difficult time with pollen and pollution, try using carnelian to see what happens for you.

Carnelian will also help you to manifest your heart's desire.

■ C H A L C E D O N Y ■

Includes: agate, bloodstone, chrysoprasus (or chrysoprase), jasper, and onyx

Found in: Australia, Brazil, China, India, USA

Named for: Chalcedony is named for Chalcedon, an ancient port near what is now modern–day Istanbul, Turkey. Chrysoprase, a.k.a. chrysoprasus, which is a gemstone variety of chalcedony, is derived from the Greek words *chrÿsós*, meaning "gold" and *prasinon*, meaning "leek" for its similar color to that vegetable.

• Bible •

And the foundations of the wall of the city were garnished with all manner of precious stones . . . the third, a chalcedony . . . Revelation 21:19

Chrysoprasus, a form of chalcedony, is also found in the Bible:

. . . the tenth, a chrysoprasus . . . Revelation 21:20

• Cayce Readings •

Chalcedony is mentioned ten times in three documents.

. . . The entity should have upon its body at all periods the blue-green chalcedony.   813-1

In my life reading you gave me in February I was instructed to wear a blue-green chalcedony stone for greater vibration. Well, there doesn't seem to be such a stone! The Zodiac Jewelry Company in New York advises me that chalcedony means blue and is a blue stone. So what do I do now? Blue-green seems to me to be the correct astrological color for me to wear as I am a Libran and dark blue is the color for Libra with green as the secondary color. The chalcedonies that I saw in Washington were a light blue.   813-1, Report #3

. . . The Reading must have meant something definite when it said blue-green chalcedony. At the next reading, we will ask just what this is and where it may be obtained and under what name . . .   813-1, Report #4

. . . the chalcedony, that it may be the color as stones or things of the nature should be about the entity in its closer activity.
1273-1

More on Chalcedony

Chalcedony is a very powerful stone composed of quartz and moganite, which is mentioned in both the Bible and the Cayce readings.

For that reason, I include the references to the quartz family here in this section.

The different varieties of chalcedony contain the same silicon dioxide form found in regular quartz crystals. For millennia, the ancient ones have used various forms of chalcedony for everything from sacred objects to talismans and good luck charms.

Because the Bible mentions chalcedony and chrysoprasus as well as other varieties, we will never know with complete certainty exactly which stones were used in biblical times.

The more and various references to the varieties of chalcedony that I see in different versions of the Bible make me know with great certainty that these stones are important and should be used and worked with for many reasons.

First, whatever variety of chalcedony you choose will be for a good reason. Whether you have a reading that prescribes a stone for you or not, you will often find yourself drawn to particular gems on a subconscious, soul level. If you are drawn to any form of chalcedony, I would imagine that would happen as a result of a past–life influence.

Ancient Rome, Italy, Medieval Europe, and Asia Minor are all past time periods that you can tap into using any of these stones.

The only other reason to be drawn to a chalcedony stone would be for physical reasons. We've discussed the calming properties of agate and the healing ability of bloodstone. Blue chalcedonies help with the thyroid and sleeping difficulties or the fear of public speaking. The pale blue chrysoprasus will help to heal the heart, more on the emotional than on the physical level. If you are suffering from a broken heart over a relationship, this is the stone for you!

Explore the varieties of these minerals, and you will be glad you did.

■ C O R A L ■

Found: Worldwide in the ocean

Named for: Coral is named for the genus *corallium*, which is New Latin for "coral."

Vedic astrology: Mars = red coral

• Bible •

No mention shall be made of coral . . . Job 28:18

Syria was thy merchant by reason of the multitude of the wares
of thy making: they occupied in thy fairs with . . . fine linen,
and coral . . . Ezekiel 27:16

• Cayce Readings •

Coral is mentioned eighty-five times in fifty-four documents.
Many of the Life Readings describe coral as a color in the aura:

A great deal of pink or coral in an individual's aura indicates
material-mindedness . . . Mars in coral and gold, with Sagittarius
indicates accomplishment—anger with many in the beginning
. . . Rings of Saturn in coral, indicates spirit entering into matter—Change . . . Coral—with a great deal of color—indicates
selfishness or a lack of self-expression . . . Mars In gold and
coral—anger.   5746-1, Report #2

Source again reminds us how to use stones, against the body:

The very red stones; as of coral, that is rather of the deep sea
variety, and when this is worn about the neck or about the
waist—or upon the arm—let it rest upon the flesh, for it will
bring quiet to the body . . . coral . . . will bring quietness in those
turmoils that have arisen within the inner self . . .
Q: Should the coral, as suggested, be any particular shape or
carving?
A: No particular shape, just so it is mounted so that the coral
itself may be upon the flesh of the body.   694-2

Ever wear about the entity rose coral. The vibrations of same,
from same, may aid in the mental as well as vibratory urge to
make those influences less of a disturbing nature which might
otherwise be disturbing.   2154-1

Q: Please give my seal and its interpretation.
A: Coral as would present itself in any form, whether as a seal
or as that preferably to be worn, rather than a life seal. Wear
coral; rose color—not red, not white, but rose coral. This is the
seal. And, as indicated, as this is made up of nature's activity

attempting to manifest, so—as ye have experienced and will experience—it is the little things in the association one with another that build those that prove to be the real experiences of life. A word, a look, a sign, may make, may undo, all of the thoughts of many.   2154-1

Several readings describe symbols to be drawn using coral as a color or used in creating symbols entities were to wear to strengthen their vibrations:

On the left . . . would be the symbol for Mercury; this being a different color, however from the Mercury below—this being a coral, or light pink . . . In the left side indicate the three hearts as a pyramid, the two upright and the third inverted—these in pink or coral.   1523-14

Coral should be about the entity at all times; worn, not as a charm, not other than the vibrations of the body as related to same. Because of the very nature of its construction, and the very activity of the soul forces of the entity, this would become a helpful influence in the experience of the entity. Hence we would wear about the body, but against the flesh . . . Through the very indications of that element as would be helpful in its experience (the coral), we find that the entity is highly sensitive to intuitive forces, spiritual aspects, spiritual imports . . . just the wearing of the coral—not as worshipfulness, but as the omen or as the charm (if one would choose to call it such) would keep the body in better attunement.   2073-2

Q: Are there any colors or jewelry that I should wear in order to have better vibrations? If so, what?
A: Any of the jewelry or ornaments that are of coral would be well; for this is—as it represents, as it is in itself of Creative Forces, or from the water itself. Red, white or coral in any form.   307-15

Upon the left side put the sign of the earth, in coral—not red, not pink, but light coral . . .   307-20

. . . First in the geological conditions surrounding this territory we find this is built up of coral and sedimentary elements . . . and there will be found first the coral formation . . .   5637-3

Saturn and Mars appear in a coral color according to Source.

. . . The coral, with a great deal of color or pomp, indicates the selfish expression in same . . .   294-204

. . . Hence we will find that trinkets, beads, corals, shells, and such things have a decided influence, and the selection and colorings of such things are in its developing years of particular interest to the entity.   324-5

Q: . . . Dreams regarding gathering of shells from the ocean . . . You will recall these dreams and interpret same, and give the lesson that is to be gained from each of these.
A: . . . The walk by the sea . . . the coral, the shells . . . some are beautiful, some are broken, some are disfigured . . . Use that thou hast in hand to make with same those beautiful in the life, in the home, in the heart of others.   538-13

Q: Is there any special jewelry that I should wear?
A: Anything that is of the nature of the coral . . .   910-4

Q: You will give a reading on Bimini Island . . . tell us if there are any treasures buried on the island . . .
A: EC: Yes, we have the land known as Bimini . . . we find this of the nature that would make the oil production very low, for this is of the coral structure in greater part . . .   996-1

From those influences we find that certain character . . . of coral, any jewelry that would be rose-colored or red, may be and would be well to be about the entity . . .   1604-1

Cayce told someone to write:

Q: What special type of story?
A: . . . anything to write about sand or coral? anything to write about sea or clouds . . . *any* of these! . . .   1731-3

> . . . coral, things of that nature become a part of the entity's ex-
> perience—these are innate or manifested by a great influence.
>   1847-1

> . . . dress of the orient . . . with chains of coral about the ankle
> and arms . . .   2522-1

> . . . activities upon . . . coral and the like, were a part of the re-
> cords . . .   3004-1

One Reading described drilling conditions in Monroe County, Florida:

> We will find in drilling there will be encountered first that of
> the sedimentary . . . with changing to thin stratums of a glass
> or coral like formations . . .   5637-4

More on Coral

Coral is an organic mineral, meaning that it is made from a living creature. It is the fossilized skeletons of marine animals, to be exact. Prized since ancient times, Arabian coral was used in the Taj Mahal.

The healing potential of coral is astonishing. Coral helps strengthen both the physical and spiritual spines and gives you the energy to stand up with courage and speak your truth.

Coral will also connect you to the wisdom of the sea. When you think about it, the ocean contains a whole universe of creatures that we can-not see with the naked eye. Although we can take scuba diving courses or watch documentary films about many underwater life forms, we will still never completely understand the sea. Beyond every camera lens, there are far deeper areas where mankind will never reach.

The vastness of the sea is like an extraterrestrial discovery, filled with creatures and life forms beyond our wildest imagination. We will never see most of them during our lifetimes. Can you imagine everything that lives under water or the vast storehouse of information those beings have for us?

Coral is a stone that will help you tap into the wisdom and connect with the energies of all the creatures of the sea. Just as an antenna serves to pull a satellite image into the television in your home, coral acts as a transmitter of oceanic wisdom.

If you are reading this book, I can only assume that you are drawn to Cayce's work as I am. Perhaps you believe that you have lived during the times of Atlantis (as I do). If the sea calls to you for any reason, you can use coral to tune into the lessons you were meant to have learned during those lifetimes.

The type of coral you choose is important. If you choose Chinese coral, which is popular and abundant, it will connect you with ancient times in Imperial China. If you select coral from the Atlantic Ocean, it will be more attuned with Atlantean energies. The Pacific corals will connect you with Lemuria and the Polynesian Islands.

A few years ago, I traveled to Belize to visit the ancient pyramids. While there, I saw its coral reef, which is the second largest in the world next to the Great Barrier Reef in Australia.

I have always been drawn to the Central and South American region, probably due to past-life influences. Because I grew up in the southwestern United States, Central and South America felt more like the transition from Lemuria to Atlantis, during the Great Shift of those times. What incredible energy!

Likewise, Australia is still on my bucket list. If you feel drawn there, the energy of the coral from that part of the world will connect you to the Great Barrier Reef and the Aboriginal energies, which are very profound.

Any coral used in meditation will connect you spiritually with whatever part of the world you wish. Use coral as a tool to help you pray for environmental protection, to strengthen your physical body, or to call upon the wisdom of the unseen life forms that share our planet under the surface of the sea.

■ C R Y S T A L ■

Found: Worldwide

Named for: Crystal is derived from the Greek word *krustallos*, which means "ice and rock crystal."

• Bible •

. . . the crystal cannot equal it . . . Job 28:17

And the likeness of the firmament upon the heads of the living creature was as the colour of the terrible crystal, stretched forth over their heads above. Ezekiel 1:22

And before the throne, there was a sea of glass like unto crystal . . . Revelation 4:6

Having the glory of God: and her light was like unto a stone most precious, even like a jasper stone, clear as crystal; Revelation 21:11

And he shewed me a pure river of water of life, clear as crystal, proceeding out of the throne of God and of the Lamb, Revelation 22:1-3

• Cayce Readings •

Named for: Crystal is mentioned 241 times in 153 documents.

Cayce gave many readings to the person identified as 440 regarding an aurascope, but I will include only one here:

> . . . Hence these set with the absence of color, or with the crystal . . .
> Q: Describe the nature of the crystal.
> A: That set both as a conductor and non-conductor in same . . . so that the activity of electronic or electrical forces in the disturbance to reception will be carried to elimination. This will require a great deal of experimentation . . .   440-6

A client requested more feedback regarding stones recommended in the Life Readings, and received this letter about crystal:

> . . . in all fairness to the results of the survey that you are conducting, I must assert that I have never been able to detect any particular influence, beneficial or detrimental, that can be traced to the presence of that stone on my being.
> I am indebted to Mr. Cayce's messages for much that I could have found in no other way. However, on your tally sheet it must be recorded that I have found no influence that can be attributed to the crystal that I carry.   2285-1, Report #4

I found this reading to be particularly fascinating based on my work with clients over the years. Many people I work with cannot feel any actual buzzing or healing occurring from the stones they carry, and yet they continue to use the stones. It is true that some of us are more sensitive to energy than others are. Just because you cannot feel anything happening with the stones does not mean that the healing is not taking place. There must have been some influence from the stone on Cayce's client identified as 2285 since the stone brought him a feeling of happiness. That is healing energy, if you ask me.

Q: Will I develop any psychic power by looking into a crystal ball?
A: If there is ever held that only that which is of the Christ-making may be presented there. The crystal offers rather the concentration of the physical powers, and thus offers many channels for the entering in of many an influence; however if it is held only in *His* name . . . *much* may be received there.
Q: Give guidance that will help me to develop this.
A: Rather presumptuous is this to take this means first, but rather before know that there has been the still small voice from within that He will guide. Then, if it is chosen for a more perfect way, place the crystal upon a background of royal purple and with subdued lights that would come from over the left shoulder—and not from the front. Then passing the hands over the ball or crystal, in such a manner as to cover the surface with the emanations of the power that is raised from the physical body by deep meditation, then look—look—and behold *His* face may appear, *His* directing spirit may lead thee; and again may there be opened the vistas of light that may guide others. And ever, when such is done, in the recesses of the heart give glory to the Father—and not to self.   275-39

Q: What is the significance of the crystal ball sent Mr. Cayce from India . . . ?
A: A means of concentration for those that allow themselves either to be possessed or to centralize their own spiritual activity through the raising of those activative forces in the physical

body known as the centers through which concentration and meditation is accentuated by the concentrated effort on *anything* that will *crystallize* same into activity. A means for some. Rather, as has been given, let the proof come from that as may be visioned in the self.   254-71

Later in another reading, someone asked about a curse on Cayce's crystal:

Q: Is the crystal ball sent Edgar Cayce from India really carrying a curse . . . ?
A: Only that that may be accredited as for one laying on of hands, or that may be blessed or may be cursed by those . . . May not a curse be turned into a blessing if it is taken in the name of the Father and the Son? . . . *know* the blessings of the face of the Christ as *He* would come into thine experience and cast away all doubt and fear; for He is nigh unto this house . . .   507-2

Here Cayce recommends that someone do crystal gazing to see visions of his past lives in India and Egypt:

. . . Gaze into a crystal, in thine own conscious moments—thou may see many of the spheres through which you, thyself, have passed. Possibly not the first, but before the fifth time they will begin to appear; for these are a portion of those same forces studied. Used—not abused—in India, as well as in Egypt.
                                                            311-2

Several readings mention "clear as crystal," as in the following when group members wanted to know what a vision meant:

Q: . . . clear as a crystal proceeding out of the throne of God and of the Lamb.
A: As the river, the water, the life represents the active flow of the purpose of the souls of men made pure in same. Then they flow with that purpose from the throne of God itself, made pure in the blood of the Lamb—which is in Jesus, the Christ, to those

who seek to know His ways.   281-37

The Source offered symbols that included crystal:

. . . an obelisk with the crystal on the top . . .   294-206

Several readings for former Atlanteans mentioned crystals:

. . . the entity was in the Atlantean land when there were the preparations of those things that had pertained to the ability for the application of appliances to the various elements known as electrical forces in the present day . . . there was the overcoming of the forces of gravity itself; and the preparations through the crystal, the mighty, the terrible crystal that made for the active principles in these . . .   519-1

Interesting to note in the last passage is the phrase "the terrible crystal," which is mentioned verbatim in Ezekiel 1:22 (see previous Bible reference).

. . . in the Atlantean land . . .
   . . . high influences of the radial activity from the rays of the sun that were turned upon the crystals into the pits that made for the connections with the internal influences of the earth, the entity through turmoil again joined with those of the Law of One . . .   263-4

. . . when the upheavals began that made for the egress of many from that city of the Poseidon land . . . the entity dwelt among those where there was the storage, as it were, of the motivative forces in nature from the great crystals that so condensed the lights, the forms, the activities, as to guide not only the ship upon the bosom of the sea but in the air and in many of those now known conveniences for man as in the transmission of the body, as in the transmission of the voice, as in the recording of those activities in what is soon to become a practical thing in so creating the vibrations as to make for television—as it is termed in the present.   813-1

... within the entity's inner self often that have almost found expression in what might be made for the crystallizing of the influences of the sun through the crystal that then controlled the motivative forces in the experience of the entity.   877-1

There are references to clients who had past lives as crystal gazers:

The entity was among those that interpreted messages that were received through the crystals and the fires that were to be the eternal fires of nature, and made for helpful forces in the experience of groups during that period.   3004-1

The entity then was a sand reader, or one who interpreted the sands in the capacity of what might be called a soothsayer, or a crystal gazer, or a star addict.   3356-1

Source described a past life in the Yucatan:

The entity . . . chose to enter as leaders in what is now called Yucatan . . . listened to the oracles that came through the stones, the crystals that were prepared for communications in what ye now know as radio.   3253-2

Atlantis

As evidenced in the Life Readings, crystals played an important role in Atlantis.

White Stone

The White Stone is a major part of the Life Readings. Often used in the same sentence as the crystal, the terms may be synonymous. In my opinion, they are two different references entirely. From what the Source tells us, this White Stone seems to be a focal point of meditation, to keep the spiritual energy balanced.

Source describes a White Stone in a ceremonial temple in Atlantis:

In that sojourn the entity was an interpreter of those influences received from the White Stone in the Temple . . .   2464-1

Q: Describe in detail the entity's work with the White Stone, and the present urges from this.

A: . . . The entity as the high priestess was the interpreter of the messages received through the concentration of the group upon the stone from which the oracle spoke from the realm of the saints (as would be termed today), or impressed upon those of that period—the group—the messages of hope, encourage-ment, endearment, and the necessity of keeping the oneness of purpose.   2464-2

Before that, the entity was in Atlantis, a priestess, an aid to an Es-Se-Ne [?], and the keeper of the white stone or that through which many of those peoples before the first destructions in Atlantis kept their accord with the universal consciousness, through the speaking to and through those activities.   5037-2

Tuaoi Stone

Cayce described another stone with ties to Atlantis, which has eluded scholars and researchers for years, the Tuaoi Stone.

Mentioned seventeen times in seven documents, I include the dis-cussion here because Cayce enthusiasts often refer to the Tuaoi as an Atlantean crystal.

Source discussed the Tuaoi during a reading in March 1942:

For this entity, then—in the center upon a board or paper—we would begin with the stone as the light of the activities in the temple in the Atlantean-Poseidon era. This might be termed the Tuaoi stone—T-u-a-o-i. This would be a six-facet stone of the height, as to proportion, with the rest of the chart as may be indicated. The stone of the Tuaoi would be opalescent while the light would be indicated from the top in the rays of the white light . . .   2072-7

And again on July 22, 1942:

Q: Going back to the Atlantean incarnation—what was the Tuaoi stone? Of what shape or form was it?

A: It was in the form of a six-sided figure, in which the light appeared as the means of communication between infinity and the finite; or the means whereby there were the communications with those forces from the outside. Later this came to mean that from which there were the radial activities guiding the various forms of transition or travel through those periods of activity of the Atlanteans.

It was set as a crystal, though in quite a different form from that used there. Do not confuse these two, then, for there were many generations of difference. It was in those periods when there was the directing of aeroplanes, or means of travel, though these in that time would travel in the air, or on the water, or under the water, just the same. Yet the force from which these were directed was in this central power station, or Tuaoi stone; which was as the beam upon which it acted . . . .

. . . First it was means and source or manner by which the powers that be made the centralization for making known to the children of men and the children of God, the directing forces or powers. Man eventually turned this into that channel for destructive forces—and it is growing towards this in the present.

2072-10

Client 2072 reflects on the reading about the Tuaoi stone:

Regarding the Tuaoi stone: it does not seem to be a gem, in the sense of something to be worn or for ornamental purposes, but rather must have been a very large block of crystal used in the Atlantean sacred temple.

. . . The Tuaoi stone was first mentioned as a symbol for my Atlantean incarnation.   2072-16, Report #13

More on Tuaoi

In the *Edgar Cayce Guide to Gemstones, Minerals, Metals, and More,* I discussed the fact that geologically speaking, the Tuaoi stone may indeed be an opal. After further study, I cannot ignore the fact that the Source says it is a crystal. Source mentioned that this Tuaoi stone has many generations of itself, which leads me to believe this stone might have been some kind of laboratory-grown crystal. Intuitively, the Tuaoi may have been the inspiration or the beginning of reverse engineering for manmade gems, including crystals and sapphires and other stones to power our computers and lights in modern times. The hexagonally shaped crystal must have packed quite a punch. From the way Source describes this Tuaoi stone, I'm reminded of today's modern medical laser technology.

Regardless of whether we will ever know the true identity of the Tuaoi stone, I believe there is something to the idea that this stone was an inspiration to modern thinkers. We had to have received that information or inspiration from somewhere. Perhaps the engineers who currently design our modern power sources experienced past lives during those ancient times and are merely channeling memories of that advanced civilization.

Cayce suggested that the Atlanteans relied heavily on programmed crystals to run their ancient cities and that a powerful, improperly used crystal eventually destroyed them. Apparently, people became greedy instead of focusing on love and harmony.

The idea that too much of a good thing can be bad comes to mind here. Mankind has many plans to try to usurp the higher power, but in the end we will reap what we sow. Many believe the discussion regarding Atlantis should remind us to exercise better behavior in our current lives.

Listening, Feeling, Knowing

Prized since ancient times, crystals are so important that we could dedicate a whole book to this one topic. Imagine if you lived long ago and you were wandering in the middle of nowhere, and a bright, transparent object materialized. You would believe—and rightly so—that this crystal was a gift from God.

Crystals are used in modern times to run watches, computers, and other electronics because they are excellent conduits or transmitters of frequency. It is not hard to imagine that this technology of know-

ing how to use crystals for our highest purpose may have originated
from the deep past in Atlantis. Twenty-first-century programmers use
crystals to make computers run faster by storing the "intention" in the
stones.

It should not come as any surprise that crystals from the earth can
be programmed and used to create anything you desire in your life.

All stones that we see today come embedded with information.
Because minerals were here long before we were, they are already
programmed to a certain extent with millions of memories from the
past, going back to the dawn of creation. Perhaps we can learn from
both the good and bad experiences in order to repeat our successes
and avoid our failures. While we may not see or feel these memories
physically, the energy is there to remind us at a soul level. Regardless
of whether they hold pleasant or unpleasant memories, there is much
to learn from the wisdom of the stones.

Lemuria

> Before this we find the entity was in that known as the Posei-
> don land, during those periods when the people had come from
> Muir, Ur, Lemuria . . .   274-1

Thanks to Edgar Cayce and the Source, much more is now known
about Lemuria and the peaceful civilization predating Atlantis, which
is referred to as Mu by indigenous peoples from ancient Polynesia.

Lemurian Seed Crystals

Speaking of the art of crystal programming and the potential wisdom
left behind from our past brings me to one of my favorite subjects, the
Lemurian Seed Crystals. I first became aware of the Seed Crystals after
writing my first book about Edgar Cayce. Once I learned more about
the Lemurians, I also found out about these special stones and wound
up writing an entire book about them.

The Lemurian Seeds are special crystals that come pre-programmed
by the ancient ones from Lemuria to transmit frequencies of healing,
hope, and planetary abundance. You can also use them to draw health,

love, or prosperity to you, as well.

The crystals are easy to spot because many of them contain striations, or lines in the stones that are similar to rings on a tree trunk. As a tree holds the wisdom of the ages in each ring that represents a year of its life, the seed crystals hold keys of consciousness. When you work with them mindfully, they will unlock the energetic healing frequencies, allowing many benefits to extend out to mankind.

Years ago, I was initiated into Transcendental Meditation. When enough people meditate together, the energy from that peaceful, prayerful space vibrates throughout the entire area where it is happening. The energy affects everyone in a positive way, even to the point of reducing crime.

In Dallas where I live, there is a magnificent Krishna temple that is one of my favorite places on earth. The monks there make beautiful food and oversee a restaurant, a gift shop, and a holy temple where people can pray. The neighborhood is not the best, but in spite of that location, the constant prayer casts a protective energy shield over that entire area. When you go there, peaceful vibrations begin to affect you the moment you turn down the street.

Lemurian Seeds are the same way. When you hold these particular crystals, they release a wonderful, peaceful kind of energy that has been left behind through the wisdom of the ages by our ancestors. I highly recommend that you try them!

Exercise for Listening to Your Crystal

Let's try to listen to a crystal from your collection to see if you can glean any information from it. If you don't have a clear quartz crystal, use whatever stone you feel guided to use.

To start, choose a crystal from your collection. It doesn't matter which one. If you are already familiar with programming, be sure to select a piece that you have not already programmed.

Listen to the stone itself in order to receive the wisdom it has for you. Crystals already have intention and programming within them. They are designed to help you understand what their programming is so that you can receive their higher information.

Close your eyes while holding the crystal in your hands. Allow your mind to open, and then be willing to accept whatever thoughts, feelings, or images you happen to receive.

Imagine that the intention set in the crystal is easily known to you. Imagine you can feel the energy of that intention, and then allow it to move into your field. Listen or allow an inner knowing about what the crystal is saying. Imagine that it is easy for you to know which parts of this information are useful for you.

How does the stone feel?

What did it tell you? You have either "heard," have a gut feeling, or can see what the stone intends for you to know at this time.

You may want to write down any information that you are receiving, especially if you are receiving directions or instructions that you might be able to use later.

You may also want to keep a notepad beside your bed in case any further information comes to you in dreams or upon awakening from sleep.

Once the desired period of time has passed, go back and review your journal. Were there any pieces of wisdom that you were able to use? If so, think about how that information helped you on your path. What lessons did you learn from your stone that you can apply to your current life?

Programming Crystals

Speaking of Atlantis, the programmed crystals caused a disaster there, according to the Source. Cayce described the power of crystals and how you can put your intentions into them. I want to discuss that activity here so that you can focus your intentions into crystals yourself.

Several years ago, I worked with a group of students in a long-term crystal-healing course over several months' time. Each week I covered a different topic, one of which was the art of programming crystals.

I conducted an experiment to show everyone how powerful crystals can be, why thoughts are things, and that consciousness is tangible. To demonstrate these ideas, I divided the class into three groups. I provided three sets of crystals, one for each team.

The first group received crystals charged with the frequency of bloodstone from India, which I programmed to bring them health. The second group received crystals programmed with rose quartz to bring feelings of love into their awareness.

The third group tried crystals infused with Apache Tear (a volcanic material found in dormant craters). I introduced the energy of protection into that set.

Keep in mind that all of these crystals looked exactly the same. Only the unseen thought forms set them apart.

The class meditated with the crystals for five minutes. Then I passed around some paper and had everyone write down his or her individual first impressions. Once the students recorded their own private thoughts on paper, each group of students discussed their crystals among themselves. After a few more minutes, I asked a team leader from each group to present the findings to the class.

Interesting but not at all surprising, for the most part, everyone perceived the underlying intentions of each set of crystals. Some people actually named the specific stones I used, such as bloodstone, while others were more attuned to the underlying energy in the crystals.

The exercise proved what metaphysicians have known for years—that our thoughts create real energy and it is important to monitor our thinking.

To clarify, when I talk about "programming" a crystal, all I really mean is setting an intention and then infusing it into your crystal.

How to Program Crystals for a Specific Purpose

Next we will discuss how you can easily program your own crystals. Instead of listening and allowing the stone to tell you what it has for you, this time you will clear your piece and ask it to go to work for you. The Atlanteans did something similar. They had a vast network of complex equipment powered by crystals on which they imposed their will.

In this instance, we are merely going to ask the crystal for help with a mundane task in our daily life.

First, find the crystal you want to use, or more importantly, the one that agrees to participate and co-create with you in this way. Select the first stone that comes to your mind.

As with all things in the natural world, once the stone appears in your mind's eye, bless it, and thank it for allowing you to use it for whatever purpose you choose. Realize that both you and this particular crystal have agreed at a soul level—and yes, the stones do indeed have souls—to complete this task together.

Once your stone selection has been decided, clear your crystal using Reiki or any other method that you choose. This clearing could consist of holding the piece in your hand and asking for the stone to set aside memories in order to assist you as a clear channel for further new information. Keep the stone in your hands or on your body until you sense a shift or until you are guided to move forward. Once your crystal is clear of all that has influenced it before, including memories of the past, then you can proceed.

You might even want to try the exercise in this section first, allowing the stone you chose to enlighten you with its wisdom before you then erase its memory to do your bidding. That way you are getting all the stone has to give. Again, ask for the stone's permission. Hold the question in your mind or say aloud, "Do you wish to work with me at this time?"

Notice a yes or no answer. Or you can use a pendulum or perform muscle testing to see whether this activity is what the stone would like.

Once you finish the clearing, you will have an opportunity to decide what energy you want to put into your crystal. Since you took some energy out of it in the clearing, you can now replace it with the proper intentions needed to complete your task.

So what do you want this crystal to do?

Do you want it to make your computer work better or clear up the picture of your TV? Do you want it to give you a good night's sleep or rid you of unwanted allergies? Would you like it to give you the courage to stand up to a bully? Would you like for your crystal to infuse you with passion, strength, peace, joy, happiness, or some other kind of well-being?

Take some time to think about what you need at this time. What do you want for your highest and best good at this moment? Use your innate wisdom to answer the question. Only you can decide what you want the crystal to do for you. Once your decision has been made, you will do the following:

1) Decide in advance what intention you will program into the crystal.

2) Hold it in one of your hands while touching it with the fingers of your other hand as you think about what you are programming it to do. For example, if you want it to bring joy, hold it in the right hand while touching the stone with the left fingers.

3) Imagine that you are sending joy through the fingers of your left hand (or vice versa) into the crystal.

4) Imagine that you can feel the joy moving into the crystal. Close your eyes and hold this sensation until you feel the energy shift.

5) Now, carry the crystal with you, and allow the intention of joy to fill your energy field as it helps you to feel more joyful.

Why Would You Want to Program Stones in the First Place?

Can you see how programming crystals and stones might help you?

Because crystals are pure, clear silicon dioxide, they can hold the energy of what you need in your life. Although you may intend to be joyful, difficult people and situations might surround you, making it more challenging for you to maintain the energy you really want. Crystals assist the energy bodies in remaining tuned into your highest good.

Experiment with programming your stones, and have some fun with this intuitive process. Believe me, it works! Remember to set your intentions, ask for what you want, allow the crystal to help you amplify that energy, and then watch your heart's desire manifest in the physical world!

■ D I A M O N D ■

Found in: Asia, Australia, Borneo, Brazil, India, South Africa
Named for: Diamond is derived from the Greek word *adámas*, which means "unbreakable or unconquerable."
Birthstone: April
Vedic astrology: Venus = diamond

• Bible •

And the second row shall be . . . a diamond. Exodus 28:18

And the second row . . . a diamond. Exodus 39:11

The sin of Judah is written with a pen of iron, and with the point
of a diamond: it is graven upon the table of their heart, and upon
the horns of your altars; Jeremiah 17:1

Thou hast been in Eden the garden of God; every precious
stone was thy covering, the sardius, topaz, and the diamond
. . . Ezekiel 28:13

• Cayce Readings •

The diamond was mentioned seventy–five times in fifty–six documents.

. . . Yet an entire mine may contain one precious diamond, and
a million people produce but one genius.   849-1, Report #11

Q: What do the diamond pieces mean . . . ?
A: Rather the diamond represents to the entity the great truth
and lesson the entity in self may gain from the study of the vision . . .   900-280

The entity was among those . . . a carver of stones . . . diamonds . . .
    As each stone indeed has the spirit—as the spirit . . . of the
diamond—it is the fire that may be in a little different vibration,
burned—so in its oppression it may bring that which fires the
imagination of those who are very selfish or it may bring peace
to the wearer. The diamond is selfish in its very nature . . . the
diamond . . . set down during those periods of activity in Egypt
as Ark-uen.   3657-1

Many readings came from people who lost diamonds and asked
Cayce for help:

Q. Is the diamond brooch, crescent shaped, in my home . . . ?
. . . Hence we find there has been in the employ . . . one who has
overstepped moral law . . . and has *removed* from the immediate
surroundings not only the brooch but coverings, clothing, and
many minor things.   428-9

And as always, many readings came from people seeking buried treasure:

> ... Do you find diamonds on or under this land in Clair County, Alabama? ...
>
> ... diamonds ... to be found rather to the north and east ...
>
> 3940-1

Source also described past lives in Egypt:

> ... in the land now known as Abyssinia ... diamond ...
>
> 294-153, Report #2
>
> ... in the upper lands of the river Nile ... diamond ...
>
> 294-148

Another member wrote to the A.R.E. in 1954 about trip to Ankor Wat and Ankor Tom in Cambodia:

> ... diamonds and rubies that had been buried in the pillars either in or around the temples (this was between the 9th and 13th centuries). Stones had occasionally been found and of course they didn't want strangers walking off with them! Our guide said that the reason for placing the stones in the foundations of the temple pillars had to do with the *vibration* and power
>
> ...   1298-1, Report #8

Regarding a study compiled for Stephen N. Green, a gem collector, in 1946, the A.R.E. sent a letter to client 1847:

> Your reading says 'Pearls and diamonds are the stones that bring vibratory reactions ...' ... Will you therefore tell us what effects or experiences you have had from these gems?
>
> 1847-1, Report #3

Edgar Cayce gave a reading for himself about a dream he had.

... There was actually a string on me ... At times it was a cord, other times a heavy rope or chain. Others it was a rope of ... diamonds ...

Q: What was the significance of the different cords?

A: ... Sometimes in cords, other times in beautiful manners, other times in dread.   294-51

At the top put the cornucopia—this in bright colors, with the fruit of the spirit poured from same. Here these figures would be twelve in number. Take these different shapes, mostly as of triangles, however, or not fully round as rolled from same. These would be indicated as brilliants, or as diamonds, or as precious stones ...   303-31

Gladys Davis wrote a letter to someone who had received a reading and subsequently told her about her personal efforts to use symbolism to become more selfless:

... the diamond expresses the mirror and the blue background my effort to become one—my desire to be selfless.

954-5, Report #1

... seven virtues—hence seven stones ... the diamond ...

533-20

Q: Is there any particular stone or stones I should wear?

A: Gold in the forms of circles or of many bangles, and the like are greater to the entity than stones; save diamonds.   852-12

Here are some additional references to diamonds from readings on Egyptian life:

... diamonds ... and all those things that made for adornment
...   1493-1

In Mercury also we find the inclinations for definite divisions of application of the mental self to material things—minerals and their attributes; that is the emotions that arise in the experience from individuals in the variations, as might be said, of carbon; in its variations between coal and a diamond—they are the same, but one is under pressure, the other is with water!   1561-1

... diamonds are the stones that bring the vibratory reactions
and the experiences in the environs of the entity.   1847-1

Cayce also described past lives in early America and China:

For the entity was among those who had come from portions
of Alabama and settled into what is now Arkansas ... the entity
was among those who panned for gold and found diamonds.
                                                                                5125-1

... Indo-China, yea the diamonds ...   5294-1

... Ye should find the diamond ... close to your body oft, for
their vibrations will keep the vibrations of the body in better attune with infinity and not with purely mental or material things
in life.   5322-1

... Ye would not give thy diamonds to children ...   5745-1

More on Diamonds

First used by Manlius (AD 16) and Pliny (AD 100), diamonds have
captured our imagination for ages.

One of the most entertaining aspects of revisiting the Life Readings
was perusing the section on diamonds. Many readings were given to
people who were coming to the Source because they wanted Cayce to
tell them where they could find a lost piece of jewelry. The Source did
describe many of these answers with accuracy, but I believe that the
extraordinary wisdom from the Source would have been better used
to pursue spiritual requests rather than mundane or materialistic ap-
peals. Nevertheless, Source faithfully delivered a considerable amount
of interesting information.

Diamonds have profound uses for healing. In fact, there are some
energy healers who use nothing but diamonds in their sessions, placing
these rarest and toughest of gems on the bodies of clients with very
successful results.

Diamonds are the mineral answer to carbon. Powerful tools for re-
defining our DNA and awakening dormant strands from past lives and

other realms, diamonds help us to fully experience the wisdom of the ages. Whether the knowledge comes from this world or other universes, our guides and helpers are attempting to work with us to improve the quality of life for everyone here on earth—if we will merely listen.

The trouble with pure diamonds is the cost. There are many ways around their expense. Years ago, I found a ring made of synthetic diamond and started wearing it around with amazing results. The stones energized me, even though they were grown in a lab. I continue to wear the ring from time to time when I need to create an energy of abundance or whenever I feel I am a little out of alignment on the etheric level.

Another way to use diamond energy without going to a jewelry store is by using Herkimer diamonds, which are beautiful and hail from the town with the same name in New York.

Herkimer diamonds are called diamonds but are actually quartz crystal, packed with a punch! Found only in and around Herkimer County and the Mohawk River Valley, they were once very prevalent. These days, more people value their significance, and Herkimer diamonds are becoming rare and hard to find. I have a favorite piece that I work with daily, especially since my Vedic astrologer prescribed diamond to me as a useful remedy.

The other reason I like diamonds is that, as an Aries, diamond is my birthstone. Does that matter? I don't think so. I find the most important aspect to consider when dealing with stones is to choose what attracts you. That said, there is much written about birthstones, and they are a big part of the collective consciousness right now. For that reason, I have included them in this book. Each stone mentioned in these pages has played a significant role in humanity since anyone can recall. Regarding birthstones, there must be some validity to the list, even if it is outside of conscious awareness. I believe we learn about our birthstones as children and are expected to resonate with them because people have told us that they are special. If you are drawn to your birthstone, regardless of the reason, you should use it.

I also enjoyed the reading the Source's statement that diamond is selfish by its very nature. Selfishness is often an attribute of Aries.

Speaking of love, once you have allowed diamonds to realign you for your highest good, they can assist in strengthening any love you have in your life. The traditional symbol of marriage, the diamond is the toughest gem on earth and believed to withstand any challenge. Diamonds will help bring that steadfast energy to any relationships you may have. Diamonds are magnificent, so what's not to love? I certainly do!

■ EMERALD ■

Found in: Afghanistan, Australia, Austria, Brazil, Columbia, Russia, South Africa, Zimbabwe
Named for: Originally from the Greek word *smaragdos*, which means "green gem," it was a term that was used by ancient peoples to describe any green stone. Emerald is a gemstone variety of the mineral beryl.
Birthstone: May
Vedic astrology: Mercury = emerald
Chinese astrology: Rat = emerald

• Bible •

And the second row shall be an emerald . . . Exodus 28:18

And the second row, an emerald . . . Exodus 39:11

. . . they occupied in thy fairs with emeralds . . . Ezekiel 27:16

Thou hast been in Eden the garden of God; every precious stone was thy covering . . . the emerald . . . Ezekiel 28:13

. . . and there was a rainbow round about the throne, in sight like unto an emerald. Revelation 4:3

. . . and the fourth, an emerald; Revelation 21:19

• Cayce Readings •

Emeralds are mentioned eight times in eight documents.

The highest vibration he has ever tested is radium at 181—the next lowest is emerald at 80. He knows of nothing between 80 and 81.   2431-1, Background #1

. . . All I know that the green of the emerald reflected the same hopes I have had for years to become of real value to broad

minded men, and to make for myself a moderate success for the
sake of my family . . .   531-9, Report #11

Cayce described someone's life in Egypt:

> . . . emeralds . . . and all those things that made for adornment
> . . .   1493-1

> Q: Does it appear that I will sell my emeralds? If so—
> A: (interrupting) This again—it is the choice to, yes, If it is *not*
> the choice to, it is not necessary in the activities of the entity—
> unless it's desirous to be used in other directions!
>
> Q: If so, how much?
> A: (With a sound or sigh of impatience) We are through!
>   1554-7

> The entity was among those set in charge of the preparations of
> the precious metals . . . a carver of stones . . . emeralds and those
> prepared for those in authority and in power.   3657-1

> . . . might the entity bring a great deal of joy . . . as a collector of
> stones that are colored . . . emeralds . . .   5294-1

More on Emerald

Until recently, I have not used emeralds much in this lifetime for
myself. Ever since a Vedic astrologer advised me not to use this stone
based on my astrological chart, I have consciously avoided it. Recently,
however, while working on this book, I began using a rough piece in
meditation.

My emerald brought up many internal visions about the famed
Emerald Tablets of Thoth, the Atlantean. These tablets, formed from
a substance created through alchemical transmutation, were emerald
green and revealed the secrets of alchemy, the art of transforming base
metals into gold.

I feel that alchemy is a spiritual, internal quest to cleanse the soul
and purify the spirit to attain a higher spiritual ideal. Gold is the symbol of ultimate perfection. I believe that rather than working with the
actual metal, we are dealing with an ideal in consciousness rather than

creating gold in the material world.

Although I recognize that alchemy also gave rise to our modern thoughts regarding chemistry—a fascinating subject in and of itself—I enjoy contemplating the spiritual aspects of alchemy.

Emeralds are a powerful stone of transformation and healing, shifting the person's inner and spiritual being from one state and transforming it into another. A carrier of the Green Ray, this stone activates the heart chakra center but goes much further than that.

You may have heard about the famed HeartMath® Institute, http://www.heartmath.com/, which does research in the recently discovered fact that your heart guides you and makes decisions for every single one of your cells. By activating the Green Ray within you, a transformation occurs that allows all cells in your body to open up to what your heart knows and feels is best for your path. The wisdom contained within your own heart, embodied in all your cells, allows you to tap into your soul's purpose in order to accomplish what the Higher Power has in mind for you. Emeralds will help you to align with your cosmic mission by aligning your being with your heart's desire, which is truly the most powerful form of knowing there is. You may do the work in the third dimension by sitting in a physical laboratory and trying to create gold, but that is not the point of the exercise. The real work occurs when you consciously choose to open yourself up to the higher wisdom available to you through the energy of the heart.

Emeralds will help you, and it is not necessary to buy an expensive gemstone. Even the lower-grade stones will work. The Green Ray is present in both types.

Part of this journey of discovery happens through your intuition and with your intention to use the stone to transform yourself. Acquire whatever kind of emerald fits your budget, and then begin to work with it. Ask the stone to reveal the proper path for your soul to follow in this lifetime.

With gently closed eyes, you can ask your questions while meditating with emeralds. Keep a journal and record your experiences. Like many spiritual quests, if you go on this journey for forty days, you will be transformed by the end of this time period. You will learn much about yourself and those around you as a result. Clarity will prevail, and you will have a new understanding of your role in the world and how best to contribute to humanity at this time.

The emerald is one of the most powerful stones of all time, connecting us to the wisdom of the great ones in Egypt as well as to many of our most powerful and influential past-life experiences. Use emerald to tap into that former awareness and bring it into the present to help the future of mankind for decades to come. Emerald is energetically believed to be a stone for personal enlightenment. Society has many troubles with the heart center and learning how to deal with the world from a heart-centered place. As a soul, once you master the arena of the heart, you are well on your way to achieving mastery over your entire life.

How to Use Your Emerald

If you or someone you love has heart trouble, it is beneficial to keep emeralds near the heart center. You can do this in one of several ways by placing the gemstone in a pocket, wearing emerald as jewelry, putting your emerald in a medicine bag, or placing the stone on the body while resting or sleeping. Regardless of how or where you use it, just having it nearby creates positive change!

▪ F L I N T ▪

Found in: Australia, China, England, France, Germany, Netherlands, Russia, USA

Named for: Flint is derived from the Old English for *flins*, which means "pebble or hard stone." It is a variety of chert, composed of microcrystalline quartz.

• Bible •

> Who led thee through that great and terrible wilderness, wherein were fiery serpents, and scorpions, and drought, where there was no water; who brought thee forth water out of the rock of flint; Deuteronomy 8:15

> He made him ride on the high places of the earth, that he might eat the increase of the fields; and he made him to suck honey out of the rock, and oil out of the flinty rock; Deuteronomy 32:13

Which turned the rock into a standing water, the flint into a fountain of waters. Psalm 114:8

Whose arrows are sharp, and all their bows bent, their horses' hoofs shall be counted like flint, and their wheels like a whirlwind: Isaiah 5:28

For the Lord God will help me; therefore shall I not be confounded: therefore have I set my face like a flint, And I know that I shall not be ashamed. Isaiah 50:7

As an adamant harder than flint have I made thy forehead: fear them not, neither be dismayed at their looks, though they be a rebellious house. Ezekiel 3:9

• Cayce Readings •

Flint is mentioned six times in six documents.

The Source discussed flint in a few Life Readings, including references to Flint, Michigan and a Flint building in Auburn, NY, which I did not include.

> . . . In Uranus, we find that the entity may be very magnanimous in some experience and then as hard as flint in another, or variable even to that of pessimism or criticism . . .   3656-1

Another reading described the sale of a company called Flint Gravel:

> Q: Will the Flint Gravel Company . . . be sold soon, and will this body lose anything on this investment?
> A: . . . they will make some money out of it.   4257-1

Another reading discussed digging a well. The questioner wanted information about how to best proceed:

> . . . Be not discouraged at even striking the hard flint formation as will be encountered in the last portion of the cap or the break that will occur . . .   5628-12

More on Flint

Flint has been used since prehistoric times to construct tools and is consequently an important stone in the history of mankind.

On the other hand, I almost didn't include the stone. I accidentally found flint while searching through the Bible and ultimately realized that I needed to cover this important topic.

For millions of years, mankind has fashioned various tools and implements using the chert and quartz compound known as flint. We've already discussed why quartz crystal and other rocks composed of silicon dioxide are important. They are sturdy materials that could be used to make vital weapons or tools during those early times.

If you are guided to work with flint, this stone will connect you to your past lives in prehistory and may help to provide healing for that energy. I believe that daily living was extremely difficult for people during that time. A constant fear of animals or the elements threatened the existence of mankind at every turn during those early days.

Working with flint will assist you in letting go of those memories at the cellular level so that you can move forward without carrying any of that primal fear into your current life. If you suffer from deep fears and do not know the cause, use flint by holding a piece during a past-life regression session. Doing so will allow you to travel safely back in time energetically to revisit those painful memories and then let them go. Releasing those memories will give you greater physical energy in the present and a renewed sense of strength and courage for all of your daily endeavors.

Often as we go about our present daily life, we are afraid of things, whether we realize it or not. There is the fear of rejection or the fear of failure—and these days our fears are usually more emotional than primal in nature. Nevertheless, we often carry deep memories of survival fears. Any fears that pale in importance to life and death matters can be crippling to our evolvement if we allow them to be.

Flint helps you to release emotional fear. It is beneficial to accept the simple reality that the fear of rejection or perhaps the documented worst fear of most people—the fear of public speaking—will not kill you. In fact, facing these fears will only make you stronger, as the saying goes. Use flint to empower your actions as you gain strength from this extremely tough stone. It will help you to transcend your limitations and become courageous in the face of any adversity.

■ G A R N E T ■

Found in: Brazil, Burma (Myanmar), China, India, Kenya, Madagascar, Russia, Sri Lanka, Turkey, USA

Named for: Garnet comes from the Latin word for grain because of rounded crystals that were considered to appear similar to pomegranate seeds. Carbuncle is from the Latin *carbunculus* for "coal or small, glowing ember."

Birthstone: January

Vedic astrology: The gemstone of Rahu = hessonite

Other varieties of garnet include:

Pyrope is derived from the Greek for "fire and eye."

Almandine originates from a town in Asia Minor. Almandine is also known as carbuncle. In early times, almost any red gem was called a carbuncle.

Spessartite was named after Spessart, a hilly, forested town in Bavaria, Germany.

Hessonite is a golden-orange variety, often called cinnamon stone.

• Bible •

> And thou shalt set in it settings of stones, even four rows of stones: the first row shall be . . . a carbuncle: this shall be the first row. Exodus 28:17

> . . . a carbuncle: this was the first row. Exodus 39:10

> . . . thy gates of carbuncles, and all thy borders of pleasant stones. Isaiah 54:12

> Thou hast been in Eden the garden of God; every precious stone was thy covering . . . the carbuncle . . . Ezekiel 28:13

• Cayce Readings •

Garnet is mentioned one time, and carbuncle is mentioned eighty-five times in sixty documents.

Garnet is only mentioned once in the Life Readings in a letter the A.R.E. received on August 15, 1946, from a member who wrote to discuss what a profound impact Cayce's reading had had on his life:

> Do not remember how I came to be in possession of a small
> stone a few months after the reading, and far from being a
> genuine ruby with its wine and carmine colors or tints, to me it
> was a 'ruby' though it could have been termed a garnet because
> of its leaning towards pomegranate tint . . .
>
> 531-9, Report #11

In terms of the Cayce readings, carbuncle is mentioned eighty-five
times in sixty documents in the readings relating to the term when it
is used to describe a boil in the skin caused by a bacterial infection.
The readings repeatedly discuss the patients in question as having poor
circulation and often pre-diabetic symptoms. Only once is carbuncle
mentioned as it related to biblical gemstones:

> . . . The entity was then of the sons of the Hittites who dealt
> with the sons of Aaron as they prepared the garments of the
> priest, and the entity supplied the various stones, especially the
> carbuncle . . .   5294-1

More on Garnet and Carbuncle

The biblical connection to garnets that were equated with the sacred pomegranate cannot be underestimated. Known as the fruit of
God himself, the Latin word *pomum* means "apple or fruit," and *granatus*
means "having many seeds or grains." In Exodus, God commanded
Moses to wear a robe with embroidered pomegranates. It is easy to
understand why the garnet has associations with biblical strength and
endurance.

Throughout the ages, garnets, which were often called carbuncles,
have been known to assist with circulation disorders, stimulating blood
flow and helping with infections and ailments of the blood. Could it be
the stones were used in ancient times to assist energetically to alleviate these symptoms? People in the Middle Ages believed that garnets
warded off infections and helped to prevent the bubonic plague from
taking hold.

Aside from its physical benefits, garnets have also been associated with passion and love. Giving a garnet as a gift has always signified dedication and commitment. Garnet also strengthens the will and helps you to fulfill your mission by increasing personal vitality and stamina, giving you the courage and energy necessary to complete even the most complex tasks.

In the past, I've reported my own experiences with the protective powers of the garnet as a tool for spiritual shielding and absorbing unwanted energies. Garnets will take on evil or malicious energies and when filled, will disperse, allowing the transmutation of dark into light. I attribute this quality to the sacred and protective nature of the stone, reminiscent of biblical times.

In other writings I have described hematite, which is the ore of iron. Incredibly, hematite absorbs negativity and will physically crack once finished with that task. Garnet is the only other stone I've seen that will do the same thing.

Once I was called to a home to do a spiritual clearing. When I do this kind of work, I usually go from room to room and then walk around the outside of the property, using Reiki and other modalities such as sage and salt to cleanse the area.

Before I left to go to the home that needed to be cleared, I was guided to wear a garnet bracelet. Once I was there, I proceeded to work from the inside out, going room to room and spending enough time in each space until I felt a physical shift in the energy.

Sure enough, I arrived at the master bathroom where I felt a thick, dense energy that was difficult to clear, so I spent some extra time there. Just when I was about to leave to go back to the living area and begin the work on the outside of the home, my garnet bracelet broke apart and fell to the floor. Strung on a thick cord, the stones were the chipped kind, so they did not disperse as I've seen happen with my hematite bracelet. In addition, the cord was strong. There was no reason for it to break other than for the same reason that hematite reacts similarly when filled with too much energy. I picked it up, put it in my pocket, and took it home. I placed it outside there, under a tree, and allowed the negative vibrations to ease off into the ground.

Had the piece been of sentimental value, I might have restrung it. Because it wasn't, I allowed the stones to remain there. Even to this day, they're buried somewhere outside of that house where they can do some good.

While you can use hematite for more mundane issues like an unco-operative co-worker or a temporary conflict with someone, garnet is a stone to use for spiritual protection.

In ancient times, people believed the garnet gave off a physical light. I agree that whether or not you can see the light emanating from the stone, garnet has a wonderful, protective energy. It will surround you with the light while protecting you against darker forces. Garnet has always been a personal favorite for me. I highly recommend that you keep a piece for use in your daily life.

■ I V O R Y ■

Found in: Africa, Egypt, Europe, Greece, India, Japan, Southeast Asia

Named for: Ivory is derived from the Latin word *ebur* for "ivory" and the ancient Egyptian word *âbu* for "elephant."

• Bible •

> Moreover the king made a great throne of ivory, and overlaid it with the best gold. 1 Kings 10:18

> For the king had at sea a navy of Tharshish with the navy of Hiram: once in three years came the navy of Tharshish, bringing gold, and silver, ivory, and apes, and peacocks. 1 Kings 10:22

> Now the rest of the acts of Ahab, and all that he did, and the ivory house which he made, and all the cities that he built, are they not written in the book of the chronicles of the kings of Israel? 1 Kings 22:39

> Moreover the king made a great throne of ivory, and overlaid it with pure gold. 2 Chronicles 9:17

> For the king's ships went to Tarshish with the servants of Huram: every three years once came the ships of Tarshish bring-ing gold, and silver, ivory, and apes, and peacocks. 2 Chronicles 9:21

All thy garments smell of myrrh, and aloes, and cassia, out of the ivory palaces, whereby they have made thee glad. Psalm 45:8

His hands are as gold rings set with the beryl: his belly is as bright ivory . . . Song of Solomon 5:14

Thy neck is as a tower of ivory; thine eyes like the fishpools in Heshbon, by the gate of Bathrabbim: thy nose is as the tower of Lebanon which looketh toward Damascus. Song of Solomon 7:4

Of the oaks of Bashan have they made thine oars; the company of the Ashurites have made thy benches of ivory, brought out of the isles of Chittim. Ezekiel 27:6

The men of Dedan were thy merchants; many isles were the merchandise of thine hand: they brought thee for a present horns of ivory and ebony. Ezekiel 27:15

And I will smite the winter house with the summer house; and the houses of ivory shall perish, and the great houses shall have an end, saith the LORD. Amos 3:15

That lie upon beds of ivory, and stretch themselves upon their couches, and eat the lambs out of the flock, and the calves out of the midst of the stall; Amos 6:4

The merchandise of gold, and silver, and precious stones, and of pearls, and fine linen, and purple, and silk, and scarlet, and all thyine [sic] wood, and all manner vessels of ivory . . . Revelation 18:12

• Cayce Readings •

Ivory is mentioned thirty-two times in thirty documents.

While many of the readings discuss the use of Ivory soap, most refer to the ivory of ancient times:

Q: If possible, please give information as to where I can find a design of King David's seal, which it was suggested that I should wear?
A: . . . It will *one* day be uncovered in Jerusalem.
Q: Of what would it best for it to be made?
A: Either of ivory . . . or ivory inlaid with gold . . .   601-5

Cayce described the symbolism of the elephant when someone described a dream:

> Q: . . . One elephant seemed to be in distress, owing to a burnt mouth, rubbed in agony on his ivory tusk.
> A: . . . elephant representing knowledge, power, incarnate in the animal kingdom . . . the rubbing on knowledge as from ivory representing the lack of understanding . . .   900-90

Someone asked about her artistic endeavors:

> . . . this may be done on ivory, cellulose or the like . . .   428-13

Source also told several people about past lives with ivory:

> . . . the entity lost and gained and became well known in those relationships with many of those in many varied lands; for whether of the spices of Ceylon or the ivory of India . . . 630-2

> Ornaments, adornments; the finer works in laces, fabrics, spun gold, silver, carved ivory and the like—these were the portions.   877-10

> . . . For there again the entity became the keeper of the exchanges of many lands . . . the ivory, the gold in the Gobi land.
>   1213-1

> Things pertaining to the arts of every nature; whether the workings in brass or in iron, or in carvings as of ivory . . .   1597-1

Cayce also recommended ivory to some clients for its vibrational benefits:

> As to stones—rather of ivory . . .   1626-1
> . . . Things overlaid with gold or ivory . . .   1847-1

Source equated ivory to the delicate beauty of certain material possessions:

... there arises the interest in beads, in those things hand carved
from ivory ...   2462-2

... building a home of beauty, that—as it were—would be
carved from ivory itself in beauty, in delicacy of expression ...
                                                                      2464-1

... the ivory from the Indo-China land, all became part of the
entity's activities ...   2560-1

Orientals, oriental trappings—the love of these is harking back
to that experience of the entity; especially those things in carvings of ivory, and the like.   2733-1

The intricate carvings ... upon ivory ... were a part of the re-
cords ...   3004-1

... temples were decorated with Ivory and gold.   3348-1

... gold and ivory and the carvings of same.   3651-1

More on Ivory

Ivory is a powerful organic gem, meaning that it comes from a living
being. Primarily obtained from elephant tusks, other sources that have
been used by indigenous peoples throughout the world are walrus,
hippopotamus, sperm whale, narwhal, wild boar, and warthog.

Ivory is now illegal in many parts of the world because of poach-
ers. Because of a good friend of mine who was born in South Africa,
I recently had the unique opportunity to see some one-of-a-kind,
antique pieces of ivory. She had saved several of her parents' carvings
from her early childhood days. My friend had also traveled the world
throughout her life and had purchased some remarkable ivory pieces
from China.

The story of ivory is a sad one. In one of my earlier books, I mentioned that the African elephant population was overflowing some
years ago, so the government there decided to allow some hunting to
thin them out. Unfortunately, when that door was opened, some chose
to abuse the privilege. In a recent segment on the television show *60
Minutes*, I learned that the elephants are again in grave danger of becoming extinct.

Why do people place such tremendous emphasis on the tusks? Many indigenous peoples have long believed in the power associated with animal spirits. Elephants are symbols of luck, and in India, the elephant-headed god, Lord Ganesh, is considered a sacred deity who brings prosperity and good fortune to those who call upon him. Elephants are also symbols of wisdom due to their exceptional memories.

The reality is that as a healing stone, most of us will not have the opportunity to work with ivory these days because of its banned status, rarity, and expense. So how can you tap into the energies of this material? Through the realm of your imagination, of course! Everything in existence on earth is available to you through meditation. If you close your eyes, relax, and seek to connect to the depths of your soul, you can access all time and space. You can truly tap into anything in the universe, and that is what we will do in the brief exercise that follows below.

As with any guided imagery journey, you can read the words below and then try to recreate it in your mind, or you can record yourself and play it back. You may have a recorder on your smartphone or other device to use if you have a few extra minutes. The effort will be well worth it because your subconscious mind loves to hear the sound of your voice!

Meditation to Call on the Healing Wisdom of Ivory

Find a comfortable chair, and then sit, relax, and close your eyes. Breathe. Breathe deeply in through your nose, exhaling through your mouth. Now take another deep breath. Exhale deeply. Very good.

With each breath, imagine feeling yourself becoming more and more relaxed.

Imagine a beam of bright white light coming down into the top of your head. Feel the light moving down through your forehead, into your eyes, your nose, and your jaw. Relax your jaw. Allow your mouth to rest, and allow any tension held there to disappear. Keep breathing in through your nose and out through your mouth. Very good.

Feel that light as it moves down your neck, relaxing, healing, and releasing any remaining tension. Allow the light to travel into your shoulders, into your arms, your elbows, your wrists, hands, and fingertips. Let go of any tension and allow all muscles to relax completely.

Next, notice the light becoming brighter and brighter as it travels down your neck, into your spine, and through your shoulder blades, healing and relaxing every muscle. Allow that light to move down, down, down your spine, through every vertebra, healing and releasing any remaining tension.

The light continues to move down, down, down to the base of your spine. Keep breathing as you allow that light to fill your lungs, traveling down through the base of your spine, into your legs, your knees, calves, ankles, and finally down through the soles of your feet.

Feel that light moving through your toes and then out from the soles of your feet. Allow the light to move all the way down to the core of the earth. Feel yourself being connected and grounded to the earth.

Allow the white light to continue moving from the top of your head, through your crown chakra, down your spine and out through the soles of your feet. Moving faster now, the light becomes so strong that it begins to pour out from your heart, creating a beautiful golden ball of light that surrounds you by about three feet in all directions. Feel the light circling around your body, healing you and protecting you. Trust that only that which is for your highest good will prevail. Very good.

Now imagine a doorway in front of you. You can see that door, feel it, or have an inner knowing that the door is there. When I count to three, go ahead and walk through the door. One: feeling more relaxed than ever before; two: circled by the golden light, feeling protected and energized; three. Step through that door and find yourself inside a beautiful room.

Take a look around. Notice what you see. Imagine that you notice how safe and secure you feel here. Very good. On the other side of the room, find a doorway there. Walk or float to that door and open it. Step outside into an open area. Notice that you are now in a beautiful place in nature.

Notice the trees. What kind are they—palm trees, evergreens? Next, check the color of the sky. Is it a sunny day? A cloudy day? What about people? Are you alone or do you see anyone there? Nice job.

Off in the distance, I want you to notice that there is an elephant. Imagine you can walk or float up to the elephant. Now notice how kind the elephant is.

Feel the power from this magnificent creature and imagine you can step right up to him. Place the palm of your hand on his tusk. Does he bend over to allow you to do so? If so, gaze into his eyes. Notice the warmth and compassion that he feels for you.

Observe the energy emitted from the elephant's tusk as you now wrap both your hands around it. Allow the energy from the ivory to move through your fingers, into your hands, up your arms, and into your heart. Allow the ivory to heal anything that needs healing at this time. You may or may not know what the ivory is working on within you, but just allow the energy to reconfigure any of your cells that may be in need of healing at this time.

Does the ivory strengthen your bones or provide calcium absorption at a deeper level? Or perhaps this experience brings you back in touch with a past-life experience that needs to be healed.

Ask the elephant if he has any messages for you at this time. Allow your elephant to reveal past lives in which you took part. What role did you play? Did you merely see elephants in your daily life, or did you interact with them?

If you need to, ask the elephant for forgiveness. Imagine that he extends grace to you at this time.

Take a deep breath, and release all energies from the past. Heal and release. Notice how much better you feel. Very good.

Now take another moment to ask your elephant what you need to know today. Breathe. Listen. Relax.

Next, I want you to imagine that you can thank your elephant for meeting with you today. He may walk back through this beautiful space and leave you now, and you will turn around and walk or float back toward the door you walked through in the beginning.

Open that door, and step inside the beautiful room. Stand there for a moment, absorb the healing energies from this place, and then feel all that you have gained from this experience of reconnecting with ivory.

If there are any other insights you may desire at this time, imagine that those thoughts are filling your head about why this journey was important to you.

When you are finished, imagine yourself moving to the door where you first entered. Walk back through the door now. Stand again where you started, feeling energized, refreshed, and better than you did before.

Very good!

When I count from five to one, you will come back into the room, feeling awake, refreshed, and better than you did before.

Five: grounded, centered, and balanced.

Four: feeling refreshed and healed, gaining much from this reconnection with ivory.

Three: driving safely and being safe in all of your activities.

Two: continuing to process this new energy throughout the night so that by tomorrow morning you are fully integrated into this new energy.

One: still surrounded by the golden ball of light, knowing that the light stays with you always, healing and protecting you, allowing only that which is for your highest good to prevail.

And . . . .you're back!

So how did you feel? Go ahead and recall the insights that were gained from your experience. Which ones can you use in the future?

I believe that we should all pray for the elephants and any other endangered species so that they may continue to grace us with their presence here on earth. As for ivory, I am confident that this material is powerful. Many of us worked with it during our past lives and no longer need to have it in our physical presence to benefit from it currently. Continue to tap into that energy, asking to draw upon your past lives, and you can gain the benefit without harming the magnificent elephants that we so love and respect.

Apatite

You may be surprised to know that ivory is composed primarily of apatite.

In 1788, the beautiful blue stone apatite was named for the Greek word *apatao*, which means "to deceive or mislead."

Composed of calcium, fluorine, and other elements, apparently apatite is indeed quite misleading. Recently used to describe an entire series of minerals, including one called carbonate–fluorapatite, it grows in long prism–like structures similar to our teeth. Not only are our teeth made of this material, but the teeth or tusks of elephants and other creatures are, also.

Because of that characteristic, apatite can be used for healing the teeth, either to strengthen or to straighten them. It's primarily found in Brazil, Austria, Madagascar, Russia, Sweden, South Africa, Mexico, Arizona, Maine, and around the regions of Ontario in Canada. Madagascar is considered by some to be part of ancient Lemuria, and for that reason, the stones from that region of the world are notable.

Apatite is beautiful to look at and also energizing in a comforting manner. In addition to those attributes, my primary interest in working with the mineral is that it is known to assist in suppressing the appetite.

I first wrote about apatite in my book *Gemstone Journeys*. The stone has a wonderfully calming energy that helps you to feel satisfied without needing anything more, especially in the area of food or drink.

There are many intricacies to the appetite. Some aspects are physical, some are mental, and others are emotional. You may crave food from physical hunger, eat or acquire things from mental hunger, or have an emotional need to fill yourself or your home.

Have you ever noticed how people shop in a mall or store? Many of us are so mesmerized by the marketing and flashing lights of retail environments these days that we leave with an overabundance of purchases that we never intended to buy. When I do that—and yes, I have done it—I typically return the superfluous items the next day.

Apatite will help you become more aware of what you are or are not acquiring so that you do so in a more conscious way, obtaining only what you actually need.

Balance is the keynote of this stone. Are you looking for more balance in your life? Do you want to give equal time and energy to the areas of body, mind, and spirit? If so, apatite is the stone for you.

Shedding the Old, Bringing on the New

Apatite is an excellent stone to use at the beginning of the year when things are new. In December and January, most of us try to shed the previous year—the good, the bad, and the ugly—and start anew. I think it is human nature to be optimistic for ourselves at this time. We hope that the New Year will be better than the last one and that everything we desire will come to us.

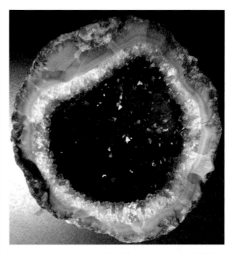

See the amethyst inside the agate? This is a good example of how the mineral kingdom works.

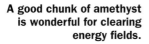

Agate rosary from Prague, Czech Republic.

A good chunk of amethyst is wonderful for clearing energy fields.

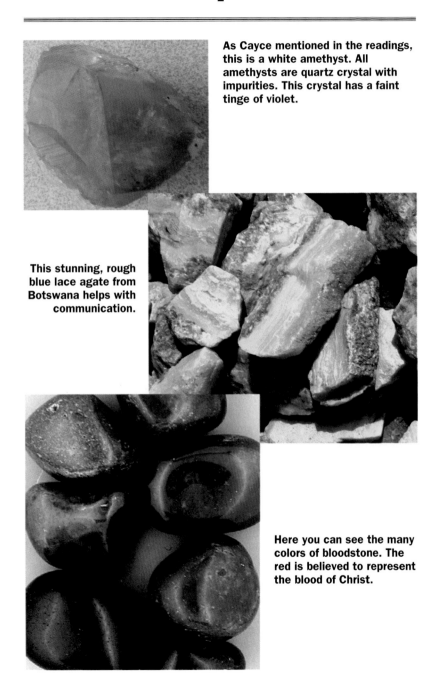

As Cayce mentioned in the readings, this is a white amethyst. All amethysts are quartz crystal with impurities. This crystal has a faint tinge of violet.

This stunning, rough blue lace agate from Botswana helps with communication.

Here you can see the many colors of bloodstone. The red is believed to represent the blood of Christ.

In this piece of polished sardonyx, it's hard to believe that these gorgeous cameos were carved from multi-layered materials.

Carnelian stimulates creativity.

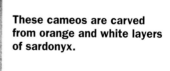

These cameos are carved from orange and white layers of sardonyx.

Chrysoprase is mentioned in the book of Revelation.

Crystals are powerful transmitters of energy and intention. In this photo, you can see that one of the stones has a yellow tint. Many of the minerals in the gem kingdom are formed from silicon dioxide, which comprises quartz. Trace elements account for differences in color.

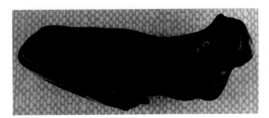

Red coral is an excellent healer that can strengthen your will.

A few tumbled stones from a mine in North Carolina: emerald, garnet, and amethyst.

An example of the beautiful, multiple-colored layers in rough emerald.

This rock shows emerald mixed with quartz, which amplifies the energy.

This stone is called a fire agate because there is a fire opal in the middle of the agate stone. Could it be the Firestone mentioned in the Cayce readings?

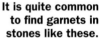

It is quite common to find garnets in stones like these.

Garnet, also known as carbuncle, will bring love and commitment into your life.

Rough and tumbled garnet.

My favorite Herkimer diamond has a tiny heart inclusion imbedded in the stone. Herkimers will activate dormant DNA strands and give you more energy.

Stunning ivory carving from China of Confucius on an auspicious red cord.

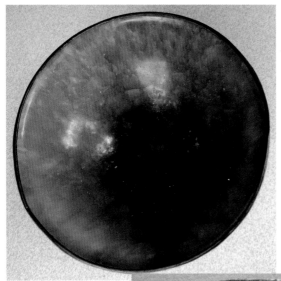

Carved by hand in China, jade is sacred to the Chinese.

Jade from a recently discovered mine in Guatemala.

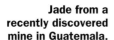

Red jasper will ground you.

Native American jasper wolf carving.

This gorgeous angel has a pearl face, a lapis lazuli body, and turquoise feet. The green arms are made from a stone called gaspeite.

Lapis is the most predominant stone in the readings, mentioned by Edgar Cayce dozens of times.

The deep blues and gold flakes make it easy to see why ancient people were so mesmerized by lapis lazuli.

Lapis lazuli in all shapes and sizes.

Hand-carved Native American bison in malachite.

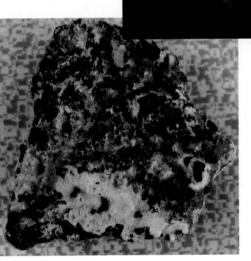

This is a typical example of the gorgeous specimens of different kinds of mixed minerals found in the Southwest. As the Source described, stones like these often have parts that contain malachite and turquoise in the same stone.

An artificially created diamond can make a flashy ring.
Some believe these stones are just as powerful to use in
healing as the real thing—and for a fraction of the price.

Marble, a symbol of steadfastness.

This is the ring I purchased in
India on the advice of a palm
reader.

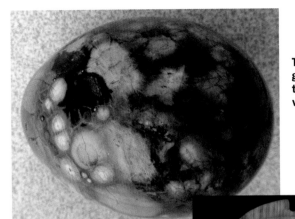

This egg is a good example of the typical brown varieties of onyx.

This "onyx" horse from Mexico is actually a form of marble known as Mexican Onyx.

The bright blue opal is one of many color varieties of this beautiful stone.

This remarkable blue agate from Oregon will help you to resolve grief.

My favorite pearl bracelet was blessed by a rabbi. It features the traditional Turkish bead to ward off the evil eye and provide spiritual protection.

These beautiful pearls are strung on pure silk string.

Natural pink rubies from India look quite different from the lab-grown, bright red variety that is sold in jewelry stores in the United States.

Sapphire carries the blue ray and will help you with communication.

Raw sardonyx is the same material used to carve cameos.

Egyptian alabaster scarabs represent the creation god Khepri, who rolled the morning sun across the sky.

The gorgeous pale blue topaz from Texas is a favorite stone for many people in the Lone Star State.

Beautiful turquoise from Arizona.

This piece shows how layers of turquoise form in sandstone in the desert over thousands of years.

My favorite agate of all time reminds me of a flying saucer. All agates have unique designs.

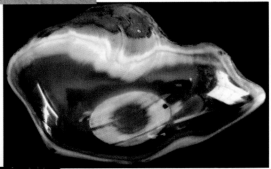

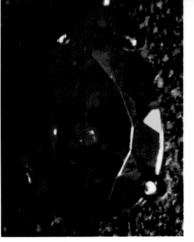

Reddish zircon is also known as hyacinth.

The challenge is that once we decide what we want based on what we lack, we often forget what is going well with the world around us and with ourselves. We often turn our full energy and attention to the one thing we lack. Whatever we focus on seems to be the only thing we need to fulfill ourselves. When we focus on what is missing, we wonder why the rest of our world, once so wonderful, is now unsatisfactory.

Apatite is a stone to use to call on the mineral kingdom for assistance in being grateful for what we already have. Apatite also helps us to obtain just what we need and nothing more. There is no need to be greedy. Nobody needs *every*thing! What we all need is a little balance. For many people, my guess is that a few small adjustments in their daily lives would elevate most situations to their maximum benefit.

Another Benefit of This Remarkable Material

As noted, apatite is primarily composed of fluorite with calcium, which I listed in my "Top Ten Healing Stones of All Time." Apatite, like fluorite, will assist your eyesight.

In the late afternoons, I often place fluorite on my eyes to energize them, and I have found it has helped me to ward off the use of glasses for many years. Eyeglasses have finally caught up with me, although primarily by choice since everyone in my writing club wears them. Nevertheless, if you want to postpone wearing glasses, these stones can help you.

Fluoride aids bone strength, and apatite works on that as well. If you or your loved one shows signs of osteoporosis, arthritis, or any other situation requiring bone strength and density, apatite can help.

■ J A D E ■

The minerals jadeite and nephrite are also recognized as jade.

Found in: Australia, Burma (Myanmar), Canada, China, Guatemala, Japan, Mexico, New Zealand, Russia, South America, Switzerland, USA

Named for: Jade is derived from the Spanish words *piedra de ijada*, which mean "loin or side stone," and the stone was believed to cure kidney and hip issues.

• Bible •

Jade, jadeite, and nephrite are not mentioned in any versions of the Bible

• Cayce Readings •

Jade is mentioned five times in four documents.

> About the entity we find unusual characters that may be called hieroglyphics. We find jade . . . unusual in their effect upon the entity . . .
> . . . the entity gave forth in those activities that make for the influence of the vibrations from jade . . . in the experience in the present.   1189-1

> Hence all forms of jade, of jewelry, of filigree, of particular odors, and the needs of such for the entity to even rest physically at times, become part of the entity's experience.   2506-1

> Q: Any special jewelry that I should wear?
> A: Anything that is jade or green . . .   2522-1

More on Jade

Although the Bible does not mention jade, and it is only cited a few times in the Life Readings, it is considered to be a sacred stone for many ancient peoples. For that reason as well as the prevalent use of jade in modern Asia, I felt it was important to include it in this book.

Jade has been valued since prehistoric times when people used this tough material for tools and weapons, which is why some still call nephrite the axe stone.

Jade is considered sacred in China and prized in the Americas. I will begin this discussion by focusing on the Central and South American regions.

I had the good fortune to meet the men who discovered a giant cave filled with jade in Guatemala several years ago. Jade resonated with the ancient ones who roamed over those lands—the Aztecs and Mayans—and I began having visions when I worked with the stone in meditation.

In fact, after that, I spent a considerable period of my life studying the Aztecs and other ancient, indigenous peoples of those areas. Now that the Mayan Calendar has officially ended, I think some of the hype and interest in that part of the world has also faded. I'm not sure what people thought would happen in 2012. Perhaps they believed the lights would go out and the world would be plunged into darkness, but that date instead marked an end to an outdated state of consciousness.

Nevertheless, there was something significant about the selection of 2012 as the end of an era. Although the ancient cultures have disappeared, there is no doubt that those early people had a considerable amount of sacred knowledge.

The Mayans, Olmecs, and Aztecs fashioned jade into sacred objects, tools, and weapons. The Aztecs issued a tax that was payable in jadeite.

During the Spanish conquest of Central and South America, jade became more valuable than gold. After conquering the Americas, the Spaniards traveled back home, and that is when jade was introduced to Europe. Prior to that time, the stone was unknown in that part of the world.

Jade received its current name from *piedra de ijada*, which translates into "stone of the side or flank" in Spanish because it was believed to cure kidney and hip issues.

The fascination with jade led to more extensive investigation, and finally in 1863, the French discovered that jadeite and nephrite were two different minerals. Presently, jade is a term that is used to describe both of these stones.

With regard to many of the old superstitions about stones and the healing potential they possess, I am inclined to accept that there is much validity to what the ancient ones believed about minerals. In this case, jade has been used to help kidney and hip issues, which for today's user would include aches and pains from arthritis, joint problems, or stiffness in general.

Discussed in other books is the fact that any green stone is helpful for pain. I've found this idea to be true across the board. What I had not previously considered was the idea of using jade as a stone for healing the kidneys.

When most of us think of jade, our minds connect immediately to China, where historically jade has been valued more than either silver or gold.

Like the Aztecs, the ancient Chinese fashioned jade into ornaments, tools, and weapons. Kings and nobility wore jade during their lifetimes, and like the Egyptians, they also took their treasures with them into the afterlife by placing these objects in their tombs. They believed jade would protect their bodies in death from decay.

Later, superstitious beliefs about jade diminished. The stones became more like a valued vehicle through which some of the sacred objects of the Ming Dynasty and others could be copied and preserved for later generations.

Jade from China, whose Chinese character is pronounced yù, was used in the Taj Mahal. The Chinese carved nephrite until the 1700's, when they began importing jadeite from Burma. The imperial jade known in China these days is the Burmese jadeite variety, which is colored emerald green from the element chromium.

Lately, I have been drawn to learn more about China and have placed that area on the top of my bucket list for future exploration. I have long believed that I travel to different parts of the world due to past-life influences, and I don't doubt that when I eventually arrive in China, I will discover something powerful there. I believe my interest in China stems from a past-life connection, and if you are attracted to Oriental carvings of jade, the artwork, or the culture in general, perhaps there is a past-life connection for you to explore, too.

Meanwhile, whether you are drawn to that area of the world or not, the fact that so many beautiful artifacts remain provides a window into the past for generations to come.

■ J A S P E R ■

Found in: Argentina, Australia, Canada, China, Egypt, India, Germany, Namibia, Russia, USA, Venezuela
Named for: Jasper means "spotted stone" and is derived from the Latin word, *iaspidis* and the Greek word, *iaspis*. Jasper is a polymorph of silicon dioxide and a variety of chalcedony.
Birthstone: Traditional birthstone for March

• Bible •

> And the fourth row . . . a jasper: they shall be set in gold in their inclosings [sic]. Exodus 28:20

And the fourth row . . . a jasper: they were inclosed [sic] in ouches of gold in their inclosings. Exodus 39:13

Thou hast been in Eden the garden of God; every precious stone was thy covering . . . and the jasper . . . the workmanship of thy tabrets and of thy pipes was prepared in thee in the day that thou wast created. Ezekiel 28:13

And he that sat was to look upon like a jasper . . . Revelation 4:3

Having the glory of God: and her light was like unto a stone most precious, even like a jasper stone . . . Revelation 21:11

And the building of the wall of it was of jasper: and the city was pure gold, like unto clear glass. Revelation 21:18

And the foundations of the wall of the city were garnished with all manner of precious stones. The first foundation was jasper . . . Revelation 21:19

• Cayce Readings •

Jasper was mentioned two times in two documents.
The Source described past lives that included jasper:

> . . . jasper and all those things that made for adornment. These were the interests . . .   1493-1

> Not in the present, but we would give that which surrounds the source, place, force that is seen here. For the walls are jasper . . .
>   5756-12

More on Jasper

A member of the quartz family, jasper is an opaque variety of chalcedony.

Jasper always reminds me of the desert in Utah. I grew up in the Southwest where jaspers are quite prevalent, particularly in Arizona, California, Utah, and Nevada. Actually, jasper is found worldwide and is one of the most common stones there is, which is one reason I have always considered it to be a healing stone with extraordinary properties. One way a stone can be helpful is simply by being available, and jasper is readily attainable for reasonable prices the world over.

Jaspers are wonderful for the stomach since they are able to assist with digestion issues and calm the area on a physical level. They also soothe mental and emotional anxiety.

Anxiety is a major cause of insomnia, and I have found that jasper is advantageous to use at night to calm the mind and help with sleep. I think these two issues are related, though, and not separate. If you're up all night worrying about a variety of problems, jasper will feel like a warm blanket and a cup of grandma's cocoa. You will feel the warm and loving embrace of this rock and be reassured that you are all right. Jasper will help you to leave the troubles of the world behind so that you can get a good night's rest.

As with all of the stones, depending on where you obtain your jasper will make an impact on how it affects you on a spiritual level. Some friends have lent me a gorgeous hand-carved jasper that is a Native American wolf fetish, complete with all the beautiful and bold reds and yellows indicative of the Southwestern varieties of this stone. Jasper, and especially this piece, has always made me feel connected to animal guides and spirits. In the dreamtime, once calmed from the soothing effects, jasper will help you connect to the spirit helpers from the animal kingdom. The jasper wolf definitely embodies that energy for me.

Red Jasper

Red Jasper is one of my personal favorites. Years ago when I first started teaching gem healing, I chose seven stones to use for opening the chakra centers of the body. While not the same as the orange ray carnelian stone, I found the jasper to be a wonderful stone for the sacral, or second, chakra, to open and balance this energy center.

My students loved it too. As with amethyst, most people resonate with red jasper because of the energetic accessibility of the stone.

Mookaite Jasper

In *Gemstone Journeys*, I described a wonderful stone called mookaite. Mookaite (which is sometimes spelled mookite in retail gemstone terminology) is nothing more than a bold orangish-red and yellow jasper that is found in Australia. Again, we should not underestimate the power of geography. Mookaite gave me visions of the aboriginal dreamtime. I began having dreams about spending time with a tribe in what seemed to be Australia—a fascinating region of the world that remains on my bucket list since I have not yet traveled there. I am eager to go there someday to connect in person with the wonderful beings I contacted in the dreamtime while using my mookaite stone.

The Aborigines are remarkably skilled in the concept of the dreamtime. Aborigines believe that all life—be it human, plant, animal, bird, or fish—is interrelated and connected to the Great Spirit ancestors of the dreamtime.

The dream continues in the spiritual lives of the people today as an interesting way to view the world. When you think about it, what is reality, anyway? Doesn't your life sometimes feel like a dream? I know that mine does.

Tapping into the wisdom of the subconscious—or collective unconsciousness, as Jung would have put it—is powerful. Mookaite will connect you to the interrelatedness of all things while simultaneously tuning you into past experiences in the regions of Australia and New Zealand.

India Jasper

I also discovered some striking pieces of jasper from India. These stones were so intricately designed that I had a hard time believing something that beautiful could come from the ground.

The stones were pale brown with dark brown circles throughout and reminded me of the henna hand designs that are prevalent in the Hindu culture. When I was in India, people offered to paint our hands wherever we went. The dyes used for this ancient art are made from ground-up henna.

The art, which is called Mehndi, is worn during auspicious or sacred occasions such as Indian weddings. The hand designs represent a form of fertility, symbolizing love and lasting union. After seeing the intricately beautiful jasper stones, I wondered if the natural world had again inspired that sacred form of art to emerge. Regardless of the kind of jasper you're drawn to, I highly recommend it for calming your nerves or releasing fears so that you can soar to your highest potential.

■LAPIS LAZULI■

Lapis is a mixture of minerals with lazurite as the main component.
Found in: Afghanistan, Angola, Burma (Myanmar), Canada, Chile, Italy, Pakistan, Russia, USA
Named for: The Latin word for "stone" is *lapis*, and *lazhward* means "azure" in Persian.
Birthstone: Traditional birthstone for December
Chinese astrology: Lapis lazuli is one of the gemstones for the Ox.

• Bible •

The King James Version of the Bible does not mention lapis. In the New International Version, lapis lazuli replaces sapphire:

> and saw the God of Israel. Under his feet was something like a pavement made of lapis lazuli, as bright blue as the sky. Exodus 24:10 (NIV)

> His arms are rods of gold set with topaz. His body is like polished ivory decorated with lapis lazuli. Song of Solomon 5:14 (NIV)

> the second row shall be turquoise, lapis lazuli . . . Exodus 28:18 (NIV)

> the second row was . . . lapis lazuli . . . Exodus 39:11 (NIV)

> lapis lazuli comes from its rocks, and its dust contains nuggets of gold. Job 28:6 (NIV)

> It cannot be bought with the gold of Ophir, with precious onyx or lapis lazuli. Job 28:16 (NIV)

> Afflicted city, lashed by storms and not comforted, I will rebuild you with stones of turquoise, your foundations with lapis lazuli. Isaiah 54:11 (NIV)

> Their princes were brighter than snow and whiter than milk . . . their appearance like lapis lazuli. Lamentations 4:7 (NIV)

> Above the vault over their heads was what looked like a throne of lapis lazuli, and high above on the throne was a figure like that

of a man. Ezekiel 1:26 (NIV)

I looked, and I saw the likeness of a throne of lapis lazuli above
the vault that was over the heads of the cherubim. Ezekiel 10:1
(NIV)

You were in Eden, the garden of God; every precious stone
adorned you: . . . lapis lazuli . . . on the day you were created
they were prepared. Ezekiel 28:13 (NIV)

• Cayce Readings •

Lapis is mentioned 110 times in forty-nine documents.

In another follow-up on the effects of stones, a letter written by Miss
Woodward to Mrs. 3416 discussed the possibility of lapis being used
to assist the thyroid:

> . . . Mr. Paul, jeweler . . . said there was an old legend indicat-
> ing that a person wearing a lapis would never have thyroid
> trouble.
> . . . stated he felt his nervous energy was greatly balanced and
> equalized by or since wearing the lapis.
>
> 3416-1, Reports #4 and #5

> We find that it would be very helpful for the entity to wear upon
> the body a piece of stone that is of the lapis lazuli variety, but
> the essence or fusion of copper; not as a charm but as a helpful
> force in the vibrations that will coordinate with the body. This
> worn as a locket or the like would be helpful.   1651-2

Some readings give more clues as to the identities of the stones that
Source recommended:

> Q: Describe in more detail the lapis stone suggested for the
> body to wear.
> A: . . . there is a blue-green stone, that is a fusion in copper
> deposits, that has the same vibration as the body; and thus is
> a helpful influence, not merely as an omen or good luck charm,
> but as the vibratory helpful force for health, for strength, for the

ability through the mental self to act upon things, conditions, decisions and activities.

Because of its softness, it will necessarily have to be encased in glass—as two crystals and this between same. May be worn around the neck, the wrist or the like. But wear it, for it will bring health and hope, and—best of all—the ability to do that so desired.   1651-2

Q: Please give my colors, stone, odors and musical notes.
A: The lapis lazuli, worn close to the body would be well for the general health of the body—and this you will have to be careful of very soon. The lapis lazuli, of course, is an erosion of copper; but encased in a glass and worn about the body would be well. The color is green. Hence, the entity should ever be as a healing influence to others when it comes about them . . .   3416-1

Study them, then, with the purpose of acquainting individuals as well as preparing same; as a pendant of the lapis lazuli or the corrosion of copper. These are well for the entity to study, as well as considering the physical, as well as mental, auras of individuals.

Before that we find the entity was in the Persian land, among those who carried the goods from one portion of the land to another . . . the lapis lazuli in Indo-China . . .   5294-1

The next entry is another letter to Mary Ann Woodard received on 04/28/57:

As to your questions regarding the lapis lazuli: Both my husband and I have oval stones . . . I sleep with mine inside my pillow case, under my pillow. There are times when I have thought I heard it singing, but apparently the singing is within my ear or myself for I have heard it other than when the stone is near me. For awhile we both taped the stone over our foreheads at night, but had no outstanding experiences of any center's activity being heightened. Rather, we find the psychic faculties sharpened only and when we study, meditate, and keep our trust and mind turned to Christ and God.   2072-16, Report #13

... Hence the ... lapis ... should be as a stone that would be about the body of the entity; not as an omen, not as a symbol; rather that the vibrations of the higher forces from these proper expressions of activities throughout the universal forces in materiality may be an aid or as a strengthening. From one, there are the emanations of high electrical forces from its copper base. From the other, there are the high electrical vibrations that emanate from its *pureness* of the higher vibration.   816-3

... The lapis lazuli stone would be well to wear about the body ... the very natures of same produce those emanations for the body in which the environ is made for keeping holy things holy and material things in their proper relationships. For it acts as it were as a storage of energies of the inner self.   880-2

Q: What is my stone?
A: ... For it is mineral rather than stone that this entity would find vibrations—the lapis lazuli or the rays from copper.
1861-16

As to stones—have near to self, wear preferably upon the body, about the neck, the lapis lazuli; this preferably encased in crystal. It will be not merely as an ornament but as strength from the emanation which will be obtained by the body always from same. For the stone is itself an emanation of vibrations of the elements that give vitality, virility, strength, and that of assurance in self.   1981-1

Q: What is my stone?
A: Lapis lazuli.   2072-10

... Keep something blue, and especially the color and emanations of the lapis lazuli; not the slick or polished nature, but of that nature that the emanations from same may give life and vitality.   2132-1

Keep the bloodstone close to the body, as combined with lapis lazuli. This if encased and worn upon the breast would bring healing, and decisions for the entity, because of the very vibrations that such create in their activity.   2282-1

Q: Is there any special jewelry or stone I should wear that would raise my vibration?
A: The lapis lazuli would be very good for the body, if it were worn in crystal next to the skin.   2376-1

Upon thy body wear the lapis lazuli, which bringeth strength to thy weakened and faltering body at times. The vibrations from these emanations, as you so well used in Egypt, may again bring in thy consciousness the awareness that life itself, health itself, cometh from the Creator.   2564-3

Q: Any color, stone or symbol for spiritual development?
A: The lapis lazuli should be the better, but this should be en-cased and worn—for this body—about the waist; not around your neck.   3053-3

In several readings, Source discussed lapis as a touchstone, defined in modern dictionaries as a test or criterion for the qualities of a thing, a standard, measure, model or pattern; or as a black siliceous stone formerly used to test the purity of gold and silver by the color of the streak produced on it by rubbing it with either metal. (http://dictionary. reference.com/browse/touchstones)

Q: You will examine the (lapis) stones which I hold, telling which is the most powerful . . .
A: The one in the center . . .
Q: This one?
A: This one.
Q: Why were these stones mentioned to me in the beginning?
A: They are as those things of old, which if followed (and the body was seeking at the time for those things) may be used as stepping-stones for the understanding of vibrations as related to the mineral forces and as to man.   440-18

More on Lapis Lazuli

Lapis is without a doubt the most important stone in the Edgar Cayce readings.

Colored by sulfur, lapis lazuli was used not only in Egypt but also in prehistoric times for jewelry. The *Epic of Gilgamesh* about a Sumerian king featured lapis, lapis adorned the Taj Mahal in India, and numerous civilizations throughout the ages treasured lapis for a variety of reasons.

Cayce suggests encasing lapis in glass or crystal, which is interesting to me. To begin with, lapis in all its forms is very delicate and might be easily damaged by the skin. In addition, it is possible that the actual resonance created by the glass or crystal would amplify the effects of the stone.

In my previous book entitled *Edgar Cayce Guide to Gemstones, Minerals, and More*, I reported on the beneficial effects of lapis on acid reflux and migraines, two ailments that Cayce stated were linked together by a common thread. Apparently, if you have chronic acid reflux, according to a Cayce reading, you might also wind up suffering from migraines. The body is connected physically and mentally, so this association makes sense.

Over the past decade, I have received numerous reports from clients and readers with stomach problems and migraine symptoms that were lessened by lapis.

Lapis lazuli has stronger connections to Egypt than any other stone mentioned in this book. It makes sense that if you find yourself inexplicably drawn to lapis, you are connected at a soul level to Egypt or the Middle Eastern regions by a past-life experience.

I traveled to Egypt many years ago and experienced one of the most remarkable and simultaneously traumatic experiences I have ever had.

The first night in Cairo, in my dreams, I heard the moaning cries of the dead. I saw weary, suffering faces in my mind. The images disturbed me so much that I spent the night tossing and turning. I woke up in a sweat, wondering how I would ever endure that part of the world for the entire length of my stay.

Fortunately, I calmed down, flew to Luxor, and had an entirely different experience. I loved the Nile valley so much that I wanted to move there. Literally! I am confident this feeling stemmed from a past-life recollection.

By the time I traveled back to Cairo several weeks later, I had grown accustomed to that energy of suffering and had made my peace with it. Intuitively, I believe that I had tapped into the dark past—a time when the pyramids were being constructed. I have had many internal visions of those times—and many dreams over the years—and when I think about those days, I do not recall them fondly.

Recently, I saw the movie *Exodus: Gods and Kings*, which was directed by Ridley Scott. While the biblical accuracy was questionable, I found that the film's scenes stirred in me similar dark memories of that ancient time.

Prior to working with the A.R.E., I had never been personally drawn to work with lapis. Perhaps I avoided the stone because it brought up the energy of the painful reminders of that ancient past that I did not want to be around or relive. From a clinical perspective, if someone consulted me with that story, I would advise him or her to work with lapis. Whenever you can move past an extremely negative reaction, you can heal the part of you that is still troubled.

Consequently, I never worked with lapis until I wrote the *Edgar Cayce Guide to Gemstones* over ten years ago. I believe that working with my special singing lapis and other pieces through these recent years has helped me to re-tune my vibrational energy and bring peace to the karma from that particular past life.

I no longer feel a negative charge when I think about Egypt. In fact, that period of history compels me more than ever to explore it.

Through the years, I've taught many gem and mineral workshops and have often come across people who have had abnormally adverse reactions to certain stones as I pass them around the group. Students have told me that certain stones burned their hands, or they have burst out in tears or fits of anger. I have seen many diverse reactions to a variety of specific stones. The frequency of a stone may have caused a major disruption to their bodies. Even though these reactions are challenging to deal with, sometimes we need to leave our comfort zone in order to raise our vibrations to the next level. The next time you happen to experience a strong reaction to a particular stone, stick with it, ride the storm out, and notice whether you feel better with an even stronger understanding afterward.

Lapis Linguis, or Azurite

The Cayce readings identify lapis linguis as azurite.

Found in: Chile, Europe, Morocco, Namibia, Russia, USA
Named for: Azure, a variation of the color blue, is derived from the Persian word, *lazhward*, meaning "stone of azure."

The next stone we will explore is the one known as lapis linguis, which has been identified as azurite. These terms are not found in any versions of the Bible.

• Cayce Readings •

Lapis linguis is mentioned twenty-three times in fifteen documents.

One of the most interesting explorations of lapis linguis and its hidden meanings and identity is found in the readings of Mr. 440:

> Q: Do you advise a trip to Arizona this winter?
> A: Be very good, and especially if you seek out some of these stones that may be found in some of these portions; for this country is full of those things in which the body is interested in these directions. Lapis lingua . . .
> Q: During which months?
> A: February and March.   440-2

Here is an interesting note that Cayce's secretary Gladys Davis made regarding the fact that Source refers to the term lingua here, which she assumed meant the plural use of the term linguis:

> Q: To what stones to you refer?
> A: The lapis lingua. (?) It's blue! . . .
> Q: Of what value is it?
> A: Of particular value to those who are interested in things psychic! . . .   440-2

> I went to the Natural History Museum but could not find a trace of the lapis lingua although there were a number of stones enclosed in case No. 25 of the Morgan Wing with the lapis lazuli. I prefer not to give these names at this time but rather to have your father identify them. They are enclosed in a glass case which makes it impossible, I should think, to hear them sing. Dad (442) is going to help me arrange to have the case opened

once we are sure which stone has been referred to in the rdgs . . .

440-3, Report #3

Still unsure of how to proceed, Mr. 440 had another reading about lapis:

> . . . to seek out the lapis lingua in the Museum of Natural History in New York. You will answer the questions which he has submitted . . .
> A: . . . the lapis—not the lapis lingua, because that is different but of the same formation, or comes from the same formation—but the lapis is there, in the hall—north side—front of the north window in the mineral division here—large blue stone. It weighs nearly a ton and has many facets, in the manner in which it was removed from the mines; is from Arizona, and the color necessary for use as instructed—may be seen by stooping below or getting the light through a portion of the upper part, though—to be sure—it's very much thicker than would be necessary for use. It's there! Not lapis linguis, but lapis!
> Q: Under what name is it catalogued? Please spell the entire name.
> A: L-a-p-i-s.
> Q: From what place in Arizona is it listed as having come from?
> A: Nearer Tucson.
> Q: Is the stone to be found in the Morgan Wing of the Natural History Museum of N.Y.?
> A: In the mineral—the general mineral division. See, there isn't such a far distance removed—only about six feet—from a stellyte (Stalactite? Selenite?) which also comes from Arizona, one of the largest in the museum. It is cinder, of course.   440-9

Mr. 440 continued to question the Source, and received a curt answer, which I find very refreshing. All of us can use intuitive advice from time to time, but at some point, we need to think for ourselves:

Q: . . . How do you explain the discrepancies in a description of
the lapis in the NY Museum of Natural History as to its weight,
color and name by which it is catalogued?
A: Discrepancies? The lapis itself, as is seen is as has been given;
that there are other minerals or other character of minerals
associated with same—Use some imagination! Or as we would
give from here some common reasoning! For, lapis was what
was sought for! That's what we're telling you all about! . . .
                                                                        440-12

Fascinated by these readings, I researched the American Museum of
Natural History, and found the photograph of the very stone that Cayce (or
the Source) talked about in the exact location he mentioned, in the general
mineral division, which is now called the Harry Frank Guggenheim Hall
of Minerals. The photograph on the main link to this hall shows, as plain
as day, what the website describes as "a 4.5 ton block of azurite–malachite
ore from Arizona." To see the photo, visit the Web site:
http://www.amnh.org/exhibitions/permanent–exhibitions/earth–and–
planetary–sciences–halls/harry–frank–guggenheim–hall–of–minerals.
    The questioner continued to gather information from the Source
regarding this stone:

Q: Spell the word lingua.
A: It has been given (See 440-2) Look it up! Do something for
yourself!
    We are through.   440-9

But Mr. 440 continued to seek answers:

Q: In relation to the lapis, I found a 9000 lbs. stone . . . Is this
the one referred to?
A: This, as we find, is the one referred to . . .
    . . . As there is in the mind of the body (440) confusions
respecting lapis and lapis linguis—it has been given the lapis
linguis is the name which was implied to touchstones, or those
used by initiates in their various ceremonial activities, and
hence gained for themselves through those forces that are seen,

as indicated, that they adhere to the activities of those bodies or associations in such a way and manner (the stones, see?) that those that are of a psychic turn may hear the emanations as retained or thrown off by influences about such stones. They are of semi-gem or semi-value to those for other than decorative or for those that have not as yet comprehended, or there has not been admitted by certain fields of activity the value of such stones in relationships to such conditions for those that are not gifted or those that are not so sensitive as to be able to hear those vibrations giving off, or the singing or talking stones ... So, in this stone lapis. Lapis linguis is that one that has been in use or in touch with those whose vibrations or emanations or auras are of such natures as to have given those vibrations in the nature that any portion of such a stone may give off that which may be heard, see?

Q: Will it being in a glass case interfere with my hearing it sing?
A: It should not interfere wholly, though it will not be heard—to be sure—through the glass as definitely as were it separated.

                                                                                     440-11

The next question reveals the true identity of the linguis:

Q: This stone contains malekite [author's note: correct spelling is malachite] and azurite. Is the lapis linguis either of these?
A: The azurite.   440-11

When describing the location of the stone, Source suggested that through the sensitive abilities of the linguis stone transmissions could be sent from one person to another, blessing or cursing them depending on the sender's intentions:

Q: Where will I find this stone in Arizona?
A: As indicated . . . in a ranch . . . Many various characters of this lapis may be found in Arizona, as may be of other stones in the same vicinity of a semi-precious value or nature, but those that

are of the greater value as the touchstones or those that may receive (we are putting it in another form or manner) a blessing and transmit same to another, or a curse and transmit same to another, will be found in the nature where the greater portion of the azurite is evidenced in the immediate vicinity.   440-11

Source discusses the best time to seek a stone at sundown. Many believe dusk is a "between time," similar to the dawn, when the world is a bit quieter so that spiritual information has a better chance of being received:

Q: Explain in detail how this entity is to tune this instrument in seeking the lapis linguis.
A: . . . Evenings will be better, or close to sundown. Why? The very nature of that being sought—it is, as may be seen from that given, the tendency for greater activity.   440-12

Q: Are these as fine specimens of lapis lingua that can be obtained?
A: As fine as may be obtained in the present for the demonstrating of, or for the use in relation to, these very things as given.
440-18

Other people received information on lapis linguis, including the following:

Hence, as we would find, the wearing of the stone lapis linguis would be as an aid in its meditative periods, and would become as a helpful influence. Not as that of lucky, but rather than as of a helpful influence towards making for the ability to make decisions in dealing with mental attributes.   1058-1

The client contacted Cayce because he could not locate the correct stone:

I cannot locate the stone 'Lapis Linguis' which I am anxious to possess. Two distraught librarians have informed me that no such stone exists, that there is an expression 'Lapsis Linguis' which means a slip of the tongue (Latin). Somebody said it must

> be 'Lapis Lazuli' which was used in the Persian and other ancient
> periods . . .   1058-1, Report #1

I checked the Latin translation mentioned above and discovered that
lapsus linguae does indeed translate to mean "slip of the tongue." Whether
that is relevant in this study remains to be seen, but it is interesting.
Cayce wrote back to Ms. 1058, saying:

> The stone 'Lapis Linguis' should be lapis Lazulis, it is a blue
> green stone, found in copper mines and the like. You will find
> a large stone of that kind at the Museum of Nat. History, have
> seen it tho not in last year or so and understand it has been put
> under glass. You can get such a stone but has to be set between
> glass, or usually does, it has the most amazing effect on me per-
> sonally and am sure if you are able to locate one you will find it
> most interesting. I hear noises when I have it near me at most
> all times.   1058-1, Report #2

Another person wanted the Source to help identify a stone:

> Q: Is the stone which I found in Alaska last summer the lapis
> linguis?
> A: Lapis Linguis (Gladys Davis notes this is her spelling, Cayce
> spelled it l-i-n-g-u-a) . . . This as we find might be said to be a
> part of that same composition referred to; for it carries that
> vibration which will give strength to the body. Well that this
> be preserved between thin layers of glass or such compositions,
> else its radiation is too great.   1931-2

> . . . For the entity should ever wear about the body the lapis la-
> zuli or the lapis linguis; for these will bring strength to the body
> through those vibrations that are brought or built in the innate
> experience of the entity from its sojourn in the Egyptian land.
>   691-1

When asked about the effects of the lapis lingua, Mr. 5294 reported:

. . . wearing of the lapis lingua. I have found that wearing it constantly about my person gives me a sense of well-being and health. It also aids in extra-sensory perception experiments.

5294-1, Report #6

Source described a life in Egypt and why the client should use lapis lingua as part of a symbol:

This should be the symbol of the entity, as should be the scarab with same; one as the amulet and the other either as a pin or about the body; as well as the lapis linguis also would bring to the entity much, if it were worn about the body, keeping low the fires of passion—from materiality that there may be greater mental and spiritual development of this entity in the experience.   559-7

Lapis Linguis and the Wonders of Azurite

Azurite has also been a favorite stone of mine for many years. I learned that the color of this stone is attributed to the sound of its name and could be used to help provide inspiration while writing. In fact, azurite is important for many reasons other than helping with writing.

I believe azurite's considerable spiritual energy and dark blue color open the throat center, allowing people to speak the truth.

Azurite also connects us to past lives and other realms of consciousness. This stone can lift up your soul to your higher calling, raise the vibrational frequencies around the body, and make it easier for your guides and spirit helpers to assist you.

An interesting way to perceive this quality is by thinking about rapport. When you go to a party, you naturally gravitate to people who are like you or to people you believe are like you. How do you figure this compatibility out? It happens through an innate feeling, by our picking up the frequency of the other person. Likewise, azurite helps you to raise and change—or step up—your frequency. You can become more aligned with higher frequency beings from other realms so that they can also more easily communicate with you.

In addition, if you are feeling bogged down with reality, azurite will help you to rise above the mundane with a broader vision of your world.

Azurite is quite delicate, though, so you will want to place it in the room where you work. Just remember not to put it on the body unless it is worn in a setting.

The Source specifically mentions the fact that the azurite can sing. I have never experienced that phenomenon with azurite, but I have a lapis lazuli stone—a deep, rich blue one—that sings. When I say "sing," I am not talking about the way we might hear a choir at church. I hear a high-pitched frequency when holding the stone up to my ear. The pitch is much higher than most sounds in our hearing range. By placing lapis close to your ear and allowing the energy frequencies of the body to tune into it, you automatically raise your vibration. It is interesting to try.

I am also inclined to believe that lapis may be an excellent stone to use when working with our beloved animal friends. Dogs in particular have an incredible sensitivity to sound and can hear noises outside our awareness. Have you ever noticed how dogs howl whenever sirens are sounding? Because of their sensitive hearing, our animal friends often suffer when they are within earshot of disruptive sounds.

If your pet is not feeling well, using stones can be of great benefit. Using lapis by placing it in the same room is beneficial, but do not keep the azurite near your animal. Place azurite nearby where your pet cannot reach it. Set your intentions for the lapis to allow the energy fields in the room and around your pet to shift to a beneficial frequency to help your pet to feel better.

In revisiting the Cayce readings in order to write this book, I decided to choose a piece of azurite to see if I could hear it sing. To my surprise, I did hear a distinctive tone. The sound was stronger than and not quite as high-pitched as the regular lapis stone's tone, but it was audible, especially since I listened to it in a quiet room during the evening. The azurite stone seemed to realign something in my etheric body. I felt at ease and peaceful, as though the stone were tuning me so that I could receive information of some kind from another realm.

Lapis Ligurius, or Malachite

Found in: Australia, China, Namibia, United States, Zambia, Zimbabwe

Named for: Malachite is derived from the Greek words *molochitis lithos* for "mallow-green stone." A variant, *Molōchē*, means "mallow," which refers to the green color of the plant, and *malakos* means "soft," which refers to the fragility of the mineral.

• Bible •

While Cayce and the Source are clear about the fact that lapis linguis is azurite, scholars continue to speculate about the identity of the other stone, lapis ligurius, which many people have presumed to be malachite. Curious, I decided to dig further into this mystery and found some interesting new information.

I researched the Cayce terms ligurius and linguis to see if they were in the Bible. In the King James Version, neither was found, but after doing a search for other translations of those terms, I discovered that ligure is mentioned twice in the King James Version:

> And the third row a ligure . . . Exodus 28:19
>
> And the third row, a ligure . . . Exodus 39:12

Further research on the translations of the term ligure yielded impressive results.

Biblically speaking, ligure is mentioned in the 21st Century King James Version of the Bible. In the American Standard Version, Amplified Bible, Common English Bible, and Contemporary English Version, ligure translates to jacinth, a reddish brown form of natural zircon.

Orange zircon, cited as ligure, is mentioned in the Complete Jewish Bible, and opal replaces ligure in the Darby Translation.

The most amazing is the Douay-Rheims 1899 American Edition (DRA), which calls the ligure the ligurius. Ligurius is the same spelling that Cayce mentioned numerous times in the readings. Although no one could figure out precisely what stone the Source was talking about, the various bibles show that ligurius is an actual term meaning "precious gem" in Latin.

Once I found this information, which I considered to be a breakthrough for this project, I decided to search the Douay-Rheims Bible to see what else I could find. Cayce lived from 1877–1945, so this version of

the Bible was certainly around during his formative and working years.
There are only two references to ligurius in Douay–Rheims (DRA):

> In the third a ligurius . . . Exodus 28:19
>
> In the third, a ligurius . . . Exodus 39:12

In the Cayce readings, the Source is clear about the fact that the
ligurius is a green copper mineral. Zircon does not have any copper
in it at all, although the stone comes in a variety of colors, including
blues and greens.

What about linguis? Linguis literally means "tongues" (hence, language) in Latin. Unfortunately, I could not find a reference to that word
in any biblical texts.

Let's look at the readings to see what the Source says about this
stone.

• Cayce Reading •

Ligurius is mentioned six times in five documents.

The primary mention of ligurius is for Mr. 1931. Source recommended the stone for his use as a protection stone and to bring about
creativity. This is also the first and only place the readings mention that
the ligurius is a green stone rather than a blue one:

> . . . the lapis ligurius (?) would bring much that will act in that
> manner as could be termed a protective influence, if kept about
> the entity. This is the green stone, you see—the crystallization
> of copper and those influences that are creative within them-
> selves.
>
> For, as indicated from the influence of the lapis ligurius,
> there is the need for not only the copper ore, that is a part of
> man's *own* development in many fields, but the need for the very
> combination of its elements as *protection* to not only the mate-
> rial benefits but the bodily forces necessary for the transmission
> of benefits through its own physical being.   1931-1

Later, same person inquired again about lapis:

> Q: Where may I find the stone lapis lazuli or lapis linguis?
> A: This is an exuding of copper. Either in the copper mines of
> the southwest, or about Superior, or in Montana.   1931-3

Mr. Green, a gem dealer from Colorado, appears in many readings as a helpful source for the stones Cayce recommended in the readings. In the case of the ligurius, he has difficulty finding it:

> Mr. Green . . . is still trying to locate the lapis ligurius but has
> yet had no luck. The names given in the Readings are in the
> language of a century ago . . . and it is difficult to find them in
> modern books. However, he is still trying. The stone I am look-
> ing for is *green* instead of the blue lapis according to the Read-
> ings . . .   1931-4, Report #6

The next mention of ligurius comes from a letter written in 1946 from Miss Mary Ann Woodward to client 1931 about the effects of the stones Cayce recommended:

> . . . Have you noticed any specific effects from the stone, lapis
> ligurius, which your reading said would be helpful to you?
>   Mr. Green . . . has mailed many kinds of copper ore, all lapis,
> for which I am very grateful. I feel sure that lapis ligurius must
> be among the many specimens that I now possess.
>   I carry a small piece of each ore on my person at all times
> and feel somewhat lazy without it (my bag). I noticed a marked
> desire to create immediately after receiving and wearing the
> lapis . . . At present, I am a Ranger in Yellowstone and have a
> wonderful chance to preach conservation . . .
>   I have heretofore been horrified at the idea of getting up
> before a group of people and talking. With the help of lapis, I
> feel quite at ease, and I am told my little talks are truly inspiring
> and original.
>   During the fire last week quite a few men were injured by fall-
> ing trees and suffered various injuries. I felt perfectly safe even

though I was assigned to the hottest district! I feel that the lapis is a great protective influence.

I also might state that my personal contacts in business and in social life are happy and congenial which I feel lapis is some-what responsible for.   1931-4, Reports #9 and #10

The true identity of lapis ligurius remains a mystery, but according to this new insight, perhaps it is indeed a type of zircon, which will be discussed later in the book.

For now, though, since the readings do mention malachite, we will discuss some of the remarkable healing properties of malachite.

Healing Properties of Malachite

Malachite is not the rarest of minerals, and most pieces that are sold these days are from Africa. I've discovered that many people are not aware of the incredibly powerful and healing potential of this banded stone. Consequently, I believe it is important for you to know more about it.

How They All Relate

Malachite has many "cousins" if you will, including lapis lazuli, azurite, and turquoise. Geologically situated in the same regions of the world, the Source tells us that all of these stones are related to one another despite a few chemical differences. Like other compounds of copper, malachite is excellent for relieving any aches and pains associated with arthritis or joint inflammation. It also aids stomach problems arising from high acidity.

The Miracle of Malachite

One of my students told me a story about her brother-in-law who needed a liver transplant. He routinely carried several malachite stones in his pocket. Although nobody expected him to live very long, she claimed that he lasted an additional seven years because of the malachite. After mentioning this report to people in my seminars and lectures, I've heard other, similar stories from people all over the country.

Malachite is the very best stone to use for conditions such as cirrhosis, liver failure or toxicity, and even hepatitis.

I often hear from people from all over North America who suffer from severe or potentially fatal medical conditions. One woman's brother was diagnosed with liver cancer and was not expected to live. He worked with malachite and has since made a remarkable turnaround. Each time he has returned to the doctor, many of the measurable "levels" that are checked regarding healthy functioning of the organs have returned to normal, and hope is on the horizon for him.

We are living in a toxic world. Unlike the days in which only heavy drinking or drug use destroyed the liver, nowadays the environmental toxicity simply from the air we breathe causes some people to become ill. Malachite will protect you from toxicity. I find this protection rather ironic when you consider the fact that the stone itself might be toxic if you were to breathe in its dust. If possible, you should place malachite in a room near you so that the vibrations can affect your space. You may carry malachite in a pocket, but don't wear it on the skin. Also, never submerge your malachite in water. It is delicate and toxic. The same goes for azurite. These are extremely fragile minerals. If you ever hold a piece of either stone in your hands, you may notice dust fragments. Therefore, you should avoid handling malachite or azurite. Nevertheless, their healing potential is extraordinary, and they can make a profound impact on any area where they are placed or stored.

Mental or Emotional Healing Properties

Malachite helps your emotional aspects by allowing you to let go of the energy called anger, which for some of us is our most powerful feeling apart from love. Anger is the emotion most directly tied to the liver, so it makes sense that if you experience anger, malachite is an excellent stone for you to use.

I don't consider myself to be an angry person, and anger is my least favorite of all emotions. Nevertheless, everyone will experience anger—as well as every other emotion that is in us—at one time or another. Some of our most significant emotional expressions come from memories carried over from past lives that are stored in our energy fields. We may not consciously understand or even perceive these thought forms in our waking life, which is one of the reasons why past-life therapy is so important. Malachite will assist you in subconsciously bringing old and deeply embedded past-life emotions to the surface. Then you may easily let go of the energy of anger or other unwanted emotions, feeling relieved and refreshed afterward.

Malachite can also help you to release negativity from the past in your present life as well as anything else that you are holding onto that no longer serves you.

One of the interesting metaphysical beliefs about cancers is that this condition may be caused by buried emotions. For example, if someone holds a grudge against someone or cannot release a disappointment, then those emotions may develop into a physical dis-ease.

When people suffer from any type of cancer, it is beneficial to release the past and learn to move forward. Malachite can help.

Spiritual Properties

Spiritually speaking, malachite can connect you to the energies of South Africa. You may benefit from the innate wisdom of that region through the ages or recall your past lives from that area.

I am always thinking about traveling. I daydream about far-off lands nearly every day! At one point, that place was South Africa.

After years of daydreaming and keeping Africa in the highest place on my bucket list, I finally went with a group of friends on a tour of South Africa. I will always remember when the plane set down for about an hour in a place called Dakar, located on the west coast. The moment we landed and I stepped off the plane, I felt the energy of the place rushing through the soles of my feet, and I knew I had arrived! The energy was extremely powerful! Something about Africa drew me in, and once I was there, I felt better in a way I cannot quite describe, only to say that the experience altered me for the better, forever.

My point is that, in spite of how much I love to travel around the world, I believe that an easier way to connect with our global consciousness is to use the gem and mineral kingdom.

Truly the cradle of civilization, it makes sense that the stones from

Africa are powerful for healing and for imparting vital energy. African malachite is certainly no exception.

How to Use Malachite in Healing

You can carry malachite with you in your pocket, or you can lay it on the body, preferably over a shirt. Place your stone on the torso or directly over the liver, located on the right side of the body toward the top of your ribs.

Exercises You Can Use When Working with Malachite

While you are working with malachite, hold it or place it on the torso. Next, ask for any unwanted resentment or energies that are no longer serving you to be lifted up and transformed into a higher purpose.

You may not feel anything at first, but just imagine that the stone is working and that those old energies are disappearing forever.

You might also like to try another powerful exercise while placing the malachite on your body. It is the cord–cutting ceremony, reminiscent of the healing rituals of ancient Hawaii.

Go ahead and lie down, or sit in a comfortable chair with your malachite nearby. Now, close your eyes. Breathe deeply, allowing each breath to lift you above the mundane world.

Imagine yourself in a comfortable place. Notice a doorway in front of you, and then imagine that either someone who needs your forgiveness or someone whom you need to forgive walks through that door.

Notice that the part of the person that shows up is his or her higher self, not the usual waking self. Imagine he is smiling at you and happy to see you.

Now go ahead and tell him anything he needs to hear. If you are angry and have never been able to express that before, go ahead, and say it now.

Once you complete this process, allow the person to speak. Imagine that he forgives you for whatever happened in the past or that he is now asking for your forgiveness.

Can you forgive and let go? Allow the energy of malachite to assist you in releasing this new energy into the space. Take your time to finish the conversation. Next, notice an energetic cord connecting your stomach or solar plexus region with his. Imagine that a gorgeous angel floats down from above with a golden pair of scissors. When you hear me count to three, your angel is going to cut that cord, releasing all past resentments and allowing you to begin anew. Ready?

One, two, three. Now, cut the cord.

Imagine that a beam of pure white light comes down from above. Feel it move into the place where that cord was cut. Feel it move through your body, around your head, neck, and shoulders, casting a protective and energizing glow around you.

Now notice your friend or loved one. Imagine that he or she is receiving this same healing. See how much lighter and brighter you feel, how much happier you are. Your friend should appear more relaxed and at peace. As you observe the newfound peace, notice how much more at ease you feel as a result of this healing.

When you are ready, imagine that your friend walks or floats back through the door, much lighter than before.

Stand there in the room feeling younger and more energized and refreshed than ever before. By the time I count to three, you will come back feeling refreshed and much better than you did before. Three: grounded, centered, and balanced; two: processing this experience in your dreams tonight so that by tomorrow morning you are fully integrated into this new energy; one: driving safely, being safe in all activities; and you are back!

How did that feel? Did you let go? Very good. You may not notice anything right away, but over the next few weeks you will find that you are more at ease in many areas of your life. Good work!

The wisdom of malachite or lapis ligurius is excellent for working miracles in your life. Don't hesitate to try it.

■ M A R B L E ■

Found in: Austria, Canada, England, Mexico, Spain, USA

Named for: Marble is derived from the Greek words, *mármaron* or *mármaros*, meaning "crystalline rock" or "shining stone." It is a carbonate mineral compound, normally consisting of calcite and dolomite.

• Bible •

Now I have prepared with all my might for the house of my God the gold for things to be made of gold, and the silver for things of silver, and the brass for things of brass, the iron for things of iron, and wood for things of wood . . . and stones to be set, glistering stones, and of divers colours, and all manner of precious stones, and marble stones in abundance. 1 Chronicles 29:2

Where were white, green, and blue, hangings, fastened with cords of fine linen and purple to silver rings and pillars of marble: the beds were of gold and silver, upon a pavement of red, and blue, and white, and black, marble. Esther 1:6

His legs are as pillars of marble, set upon sockets of fine gold: his countenance is as Lebanon, excellent as the cedars. Song of Solomon 5:15

. . . all manner vessels of most precious wood, and of brass, and iron, and marble, Revelation 18:12

• Cayce Reading •

Marble is mentioned 140 times in ninety-two documents.

Although there are numerous references to marble in the Life Readings, many of these were given to someone who wanted to make imitation marble. I have omitted several other references regarding the Georgia Marble Company.

As always, Source had much to share about this ancient material, describing marble in a past life that took place in Atlantis:

In the one before this we find in the Atlantean rule. The entity then one of high authority, being then the ruler in that land . . . The urge from this is toward those of the arts and specially that of the work in those of stone, marble, granite, or of elemental forces in same . . .   779-9

Q: I turned in bed and beheld before me a statue in marble . . . It was a headless statue, such as are represented in marble of the Greek god Zeus . . .

A: . . . two elements are presented to the entity, and the subconscious forces of the entity reason with self that back of the statue there must be that which would form or produce same . . .

900-294

. . . various forms of expression of individual ideas or ideals, in cast, in marble, in the elements that were used in same in the period, occupied that of the developing portion of the entity's experience . . .   275-25

Before this we find the entity was in the Grecian land; beautiful of body, of mind, of abilities to aid many in gaining an apprecia-tion of music as was depicted by those in the pastoral scenes, by those who would put into marble and into paintings their appreciation of such beauties in those early periods.   1823-1

. . . the entity . . . gained the understanding of that attempted to be presented in figures . . . from marble, from iron, from brass, gold and precious stone . . .   2108-1

In the first, we find in that the love or the inanimate forces as express themselves in their inner being concerning those things that have to do with the beautiful, in those of marble or of cut stone . . .   2790-2

Cayce gave a reading to someone who was in Alexandria, Egypt during the destruction of the library there:

The entity may, through the present experience, desire with self much of the wisdom which was lost through the destruction of manuscripts in that particular period, and these are the fears which arise in the entity from the marble mobbed rule. Thus ever the lawyer, or justice principle, is a part of the conscious-ness . . .   5254-1

More on Marble

When traveling in Mexico these days, there are many "onyx" prod-ucts for sale—everything from chess boards to figurines and statues. These carbonate rocks look like onyx but are not that material. The locals call it Mexican onyx. Geologically speaking, the two stones are not the same. Real onyx is a banded variety of chalcedony, as is agate. The Mexican carvings are made from marble. Regardless of what you call them, the stones are beautiful and are fashioned into souvenirs such as chess pieces, animal figures, pieces of fruit, and bowls.

If you asked me to describe my personal experience in working with marble stones for healing, I would have told you initially that I haven't used marble very much. That isn't actually the case. I've had a marble piece in my possession for so long that I forgot all about it because it has been such an ever-present part of my surroundings. Among all the stones that have come and gone from my life, this marble piece remains with me to this day. Years ago a friend gave me a gigantic marble sphere. Although it was a nice gesture, and it is certainly a beautiful piece, I had no idea what to do with it. For that reason, I have tried without any luck over the years to release this piece to others. Because of the large size, the marble sphere has remained with me.

Interestingly, one of the attributes of marble is steadfast loyalty. If you want to build a solid foundation for your life and establish greater stability, marble will ground you with a feeling of lasting pleasure and reliability.

There is no coincidence that the elegant busts of famous people in Italy and Greece have been carved from marble throughout history. For one thing, that material is in abundance there, and for another, the marble allows the image of that person to be deeply ingrained in our minds in the most positive light possible.

Any situation needing some positive spin control will benefit from the use of marble. Additionally, marble countertops and flooring in homes are examples of the fact that marble is a stone of abundance, re-minding you to indulge yourself in life's finer things once in a while.

I'm not surprised to see references to Atlantis and marble in the Cayce readings. At a soul level, I often think about Atlantis. The im-age that always comes to mind is an open-air home with a gorgeous marble-floored outdoor patio next to pools of water brimming with dolphins that come to eat from my hands. The architecture is similar to Greece, with columns holding up the structure. Several raised walk-ways allow people to walk out into the middle of the turquoise water as if they are floating. Elegance, beauty, and durability are attributes of this stone. But just as Atlantis didn't last due to the imbalances of the material desires over spiritual aspects, marble reminds us of past mistakes and the importance of bringing balance into all areas of our lives. It is certainly nice to live like a king every now and then. It is also important to remain ever mindful that being kind to others and living a good, spiritual life should take precedence over worldly concerns. Nevertheless, we inhabit a planet and are here to have a physical and material experience. Sometimes we can go too far off in the other direction. For example, we cannot serve our fellow man by staying in meditation all day long (unless, of course, we're monks or nuns). Most of us are not in the priesthood in this incarnation, so it is best to strive for some balance somewhere between the spiritual and the mundane world. Marble will help.

The other aspect of marble is its connection to Greece and Italy. If you are drawn to that part of the world, having a marble bust of an historical figure may trigger your memories of those early times. Many innovations and creative inventions that influenced history, particularly in the world of philosophy, began in Greece. Marble will draw out your inner philosopher and allow you to recall your former brilliance. It will help to bring that wisdom into the present for the betterment of humanity.

White marble from Jodhpur was used in the Taj Mahal in India, and the walls of the palace were also made from marble. You may find that the stone draws you into those incarnations as well.

The Hindu religion and Indian culture are fascinating. The people of India believe that we have lived before our current life and that there are consequences for one's actions. They work to be peaceful in their inner world and accept what is theirs to do in this lifetime. Marble represents a form of purity and perfection, a state of nirvana that we can all strive to attain.

■MOONSTONE■

Found in: Australia, Brazil, Burma, Europe, India, Madagascar, Sri Lanka, USA

Named for: Moonstone is composed of feldspar, which is derived from the German words *feld* for "field," *fels* for "rock," and *spat* for "chip."

Birthstone: June

Chinese astrology: Pig = moonstone

• Bible •

The Bible does not mention moonstone or feldspar.

• Cayce Readings •

Moonstone is mentioned thirteen times in eleven documents.

> . . . moonstone should be stones about the body or entity oft . . .
>> 1406-1

> The moonstone . . . should be as an amulet, either about the neck or as a ring, or worn upon the person. . . .
> From the astrological aspects, we find there was a sojourn upon the moon.
> Hence, the moon is an active influence of the entity, and *do not* ever sleep with the moon shining upon the face.
> . . . for the moon and the sun are the ruling of the emotions . . .
>> 1401-1

> Wear the others . . . with moonstone or the like as rings or amulets or anklets; but never those upon the neck or in the ears—rather upon the extremities; for they will make for the bringing out—in the experiences of those the entity meets—or those very colors and vibrations that have been indicated to which the entity is so sensitive.   1406-1

> . . . might the entity bring a great deal of joy, of harmony into the experience of those with whom he might work . . . moonstone . . .
> . . . the moonstone might find that it would bring peace . . .
>> 5294-1

Cayce described a dream he had:

> . . . moonstone box . . . It seemed that the material manifestation of my physical and mental self was in the box . . .
>> 257-130, Report #1

... beneficial effect of ... moonstone; colors mingled in shades of gray, modes, blue and the like, or decided colors; psychic development from within rather than being directed from anyone from outside.   276-2, Report #5

Q: What stones have a beneficial effect on body?
A: ... moonstone.   276-5

Q: What is the entity's stone ... ?
A: ... the stone would be ... moonstone.   282-7

... influences that may bring the greater force about the body, the moonstone ...   608-7

... the moonstone ... well to have about the body.   1037-1

The moonstone ... should be as an amulet, either about the neck or as a ring, or worn upon the person.   1401-1

In the material things—wear as an ornament, preferably a ring, the moonstone ... vibrations are in accord with that to keep thy animation in accord with the best thou mayest accomplish.
                                                                 1620-2

... wear the moonstone close to your body, or on your body. It will give strength, and it will keep that which is nearest to you closer to you; not as an omen but as a part of your mental and spiritual consciousness ...   5125-1

... The same individual wearing or having in the apparel the moonstone might find that it would bring peace, harmony and those tendencies toward spiritual things ...   5294-1

More on Moonstone

Even though the Bible does not include moonstone, it was mentioned numerous times by the Source, who attributed the stone with bringing feelings of peace, security, and beauty to the wearers.

Recently I completed another book on stones called *Multidimensional Minerals* that prominently features moonstone and labradorite, both minerals of the feldspar group.

There is something magical about these stones. They provide interesting windows to other worlds. By windows, I mean physical mirrors that can be used to peer at spirit guides who appear with messages for us.

Moonstone varieties differ. Some pieces have a fleshy appearance that looks like skin, while other rainbow varieties have translucent layers of blue and green undertones that can be used for gazing.

If you need protection in travel, moonstone is helpful. The belief of protection derived from ancient times especially for people who traveled at night or when the moon was shining upon the water. As the name implies, moonstones connect you to the physical moon and the emotional side of life.

When I first started working in the metaphysical field, I attended numerous psychic fairs at stores. I began teaching people about the uses of stones at that time.

Since you are reading this book, perhaps you have shopped in metaphysical or New Age stores. If so, you might have noticed certain stones that sell regularly, often fashioned into jewelry. Moonstone is among the most popular of those choices.

Moonstone, as its name suggests, connects you with the energy of the moon, the lunar, or the feminine side of your nature. We have within ourselves both masculine and feminine energies.

You will feel your best when you learn to balance these masculine and feminine—or Yin and Yang—energies within you. The sun is considered to be a masculine energy—aggressive and dominating. The moon is feminine—receptive, allowing, and attracting. Lunar energy will help you to draw things to yourself rather than having to attain them.

When you go into a metaphysical shop, the psychic readers will attempt to tap into that lunar, receptive part of themselves in order to give you answers to your questions about love, health, money, or more. The stones they wear or work with actually facilitate their ability to receive information. They open their energy fields and receive information to pass on to you. Moonstone is a wonderful tool for enhancing this process.

As the Source described in the readings, moonstone is also excellent for helping to develop psychic abilities. The moonstone allows you to actively open your fields in order to receive more intuitive information. You can allow the energy of moonstone to help you to open your third eye center. You may also use it as a gazing stone to see images.

Moonstone also helps you to commune with lost loved ones, receive guidance from guides and helpers, or gain inspiration.

You may also want to try placing a moonstone on the center of your forehead. If you place the stone there and then take a chakra power nap for about twenty minutes, you may feel the stone start to vibrate. Moonstone helps to open the third eye center so that you can receive greater intuitive guidance.

We all have intuitive abilities, but often our world is so hectic that we have a difficult time tuning into various issues or ourselves. Moonstone will help you to receive inner guidance by quieting down the outer world.

■ONYX AND SARDONYX■

Onyx is formed from bands of chalcedony, and sardonyx is a variant.

Found in: Australia, Canada, China, India, Russia, USA

Named for: Onyx is derived from a Greek word that means "fingernail."

• Bible •

Onyx and chalcedony are both mentioned in the Bible.

Onyx is recorded eleven times:

And the gold of that land is good: there is bdellium and the onyx stone. Genesis 2:12

Onyx stones, and stones to be set in the ephod, and in the breastplate. Exodus 25:7

And thou shalt take two onyx stones, and grave on them the names of the children of Israel: Exodus 28:9

And the fourth row . . . an onyx . . . they shall be set in gold in their inclosings. Exodus 28:20

. . . and onyx stones, and stones to be set for the ephod, and for the breastplate. Exodus 35:9

And the rulers brought onyx stones, and stones to be set, for the ephod, and for the breastplate; Exodus 35:27

And they wrought onyx stones enclosed in ouches of gold, graven, as signets are graven, with the names of the children of Israel. Exodus 39:6

And the fourth row . . . an onyx . . . enclosed in ouches of gold in their settings. Exodus 39:13

Now I have prepared with all my might for the house of my God the gold for things to be made of gold, and the silver for things of silver, and the brass for things of brass, the iron for things of iron, and wood for things of wood; onyx stones, and stones to be set, glistering stones, and of divers colours, and all manner of precious stones, and marble stones in abundance. 1 Chronicles 29:2

It cannot be valued with the gold of Ophir, with the precious onyx . . . Job 28:16

Thou hast been in Eden the garden of God; every precious stone was thy covering . . . the onyx . . . Ezekiel 28:13

The following reading for sardonyx, a variant of onyx, appears as onyx in the American Standard Version of the Bible:

. . . the fifth, sardonyx . . . Revelation 21:20 (ASV)

• Cayce Readings •

Sardonyx is mentioned two times in two documents.

Dealers in semi-precious stones should be able to secure the sardonyx stones for him . . .   1528-1, Report #1

Well that there be carried on the person the sardonyx stone (that is in its semi-precious state); either in statuettes, pins, buttons, or a piece of same carried. Not as a protection, but rather for the vibratory forces that influence the choices made by the mental forces of the entity itself. Statuettes, frames or the like are well. Much of the same vibrations may be obtained from using those combinations of stone made from the soya bean;

that may act in much the same capacity. Figures made of same
are well to have about the entity's *sleeping* quarters or abode.
1528-1

Onyx is mentioned fifteen times in fourteen documents.

Q: To what color, symbol or stone does entity vibrate best?
A: . . . onyx, and as to colors—the radiation of colors from . . .
onyx.   2542-1

. . . in the upper lands of the river Nile, there were those mines
of precious stones—as onyx . . .   294-153, Report #2 and also
294-148

In the temple were to be found enormous semi-circular columns
of onyx . . .   364-13

Cayce had a dream during a reading:

. . . I saw an altar built under a large tree—very beautiful setting.
A priest was offering incense or burning sacrifice; altar made of
onyx, priest dressed in brocades.   4293-1, Report #1

Cayce gave a reading for another person who lived near the Nile:

The furnishings may be surmised from the fact that the most
beautiful things from each land were gathered there; gold, silver,
onyx, iron, brass, silk, satins, linen.   281-25

. . . there is a whole civilization above entity's temple; yea, even
its bed, which is almost of pure gold and onyx.   873-1

Hence . . . the onyx . . . stones or things of the nature should be
about the entity in its closer activity.   1273-1

. . . those things that might be turned into adornments . . . onyx . . .
these were the interests, these were the activities of the entity . . .
1493-1

Again, Cayce gave advice to mineral speculators regarding the value of land and potential discoveries on the property:

> . . . Now the upper stratas we will find from tree entrance are
> hard, close-grained sand, some showing . . . onyx . . .   4398-3

More on Onyx

Onyx can be used to aid in grief recovery and would be a perfect stone to wear to a funeral or while in mourning. Interestingly, the word *onyx*, or *onychis*, means "box of unguent" in Latin, which brings to mind something that might be used at a funeral. Queen Victoria of England popularized the onyx when she wore the stone after the death of her beloved Prince Albert. The Victorian Age in England was considered very prim and proper, and to this day, the energy of onyx can produce that kind of image for those who wear it.

If you had to go to court, for example, onyx would be the perfect stone to wear to impart an innocent, chaste energy in order to turn the court's favor to your cause.

One of my first rings was an onyx with a tiny diamond. I wore it daily and found that it kept me grounded and appeared to repel negativity.

Onyx is beneficial to use in any situation in which you want to show your best light. Use onyx for job interviews, classes or other important meetings at school, or for whenever it's important to persuade any group of people to be on your side.

More on Sardonyx

One of the favorite periods in history that I love to read about is the reign of Queen Elizabeth I. I've spent too many hours to count reading delightful books about her life. I've also watched every film I can get my hands on about this period in history, almost to the point of obsession. Do I have a past–life connection with that time period? Perhaps!

There are many interesting stories about the Queen and how she handled herself with numerous suitors over the course of her lifetime. She never married because she believed that to do so would be her undoing, both politically and physically. There were numerous plots against her life. She deserves a lot of credit for keeping herself alive and for thriving as the leader of such a mighty empire.

One of the most interesting aspects of her story is her alleged romance with the married 2nd Earl of Essex, Robert Devereux, who was considered to be her favorite at court. The Queen gave the Earl a sardonyx ring set in gold as a token of her affection.

During the Renaissance, people believed that sardonyx helped the wearer to appear more sophisticated with speech. In the Queen's court, good communication would certainly have been important for everyone.

Shoham Stones

After researching the various stones in the breastplate of the high priest that is mentioned in the Bible and the Cayce readings, I discovered that onyx had a far greater importance in biblical times than I had first realized. In the breastplate, there are two stones worn by the priest, one on each shoulder, which have the names of the twelve tribes of Israel inscribed on them, and there are six per stone. (From: http://tthemessiahssecret.blogspot.com/2011/04/messiahs-secret-jesus-light-of-world.html)

These so-called Remembrance Stones reminded the Creator of the children of Israel so that he would have mercy on them. Jewish scholars believe that these two stones, called Shoham stones, were onyx. *Shoham* in Hebrew literally translates to the word "onyx."

The Jewish historian Josephus, who lived from 37–100 AD, had access to the breastplate. He confirmed that these stones were onyx in the writings he left behind.

Pebbles for the Dead

In the Jewish faith, there is a fascinating custom of placing tiny pebbles on people's graves, which is a gesture similar to leaving a calling card when visiting someone. Leaving a stone is their way to say hello and pay one's respects to the dead.

I saw this custom firsthand when I visited the Jewish Museum in Prague, Czech Republic, a few years ago. The burial site for one of the most famous Jewish Rabbis, Judah Loew ben Bezalel (c. 1520–1609) is there, and I wanted to see the place for myself. Rabbi Loew wrote many books on law, philosophy, and morality. I wandered through the ancient Jewish cemetery located in the Old City Centre and was stunned to see the primeval graves protruding from the ground in an eerie, haphazard way. The grounds are profoundly quiet, despite the noisy city streets beyond the walls. I walked slowly, careful not to disturb any resting places. The area is filled to the brim with graves, and I began noticing tiny little rocks on the top of the headstones. Wondering what it meant, I stood still with my back against a wall for some time, watching and observing people as they visited to pay their respects. Many placed stones on the graves. When I finally arrived at Rabbi Loew's tombstone, I found a tiny rock on the ground, not more than a millimeter in diameter, and placed it on his headstone. I felt as though I were saying, "Hi! I'm here!" It felt like I left a little bit of myself on the site. Sure enough, once I got home and researched the custom further, I discovered that leaving a stone on a gravesite is a sign of respect.

▪ O P A L ▪

Found in: Argentina, Brazil, Canada, China, Czech Republic, Egypt, Ethiopia, Germany, USA
Named for: Opal is derived from *úpala*, the Sanskrit word for "precious stone."
Birthstone: October
Chinese astrology: Snake = opal

• Bible •

There are no references to opal in the King James Version; however, scholars from the Temple Institute in Jerusalem believe that opal is the actual identity of one of the stones in the breastplate of the high priest.

and in the third row, an opal, an agate, and an amethyst; Exodus 28:19 (Darby Bible Translation)

• Cayce Readings •

Opal is mentioned forty-five times in twenty-three documents.

Cayce described a costume someone wore in a prior incarnation and then warned against wearing the opal:

> . . . serpent headgear but with the sunburst of opal . . .
> Q: Any special jewelry I should wear?
> A: . . . not opals, however. Though these appear in the seal, they are—as self—sometimes fickle.   2522-1

> Q: Will wearing opals by one who does not have them as a birth stone signify ill omens for that person?
> A: No, opals will be helpful if there is kept the correct attitude, for it will enable the entity to hold on to self or to prevent those who would be angry from flying off the handle too much.
>   4006-1

> . . . Also in the land now known as Abyssinia . . . in the upper lands of the river Nile, there were those mines of precious stones . . . opal . . .   294-153, Report #2

There are many readings about mineral rights near Yuma, Arizona, including this one:

> Q: Give exact location and depth below surface.
> A: We have given the exact location, you see, here on the ridge . . . in North and Easterly direction . . . opal . . .   195-7

> Q: What stones have a beneficial effect on body?
> A: Opal . . .   276-5

> Hence the colors that will influence the developing years for the entity will be blue and yellow, or shades and tones of these particular colors with the opal . . .   314-1

> Q: To what musical notes and colors do I vibrate?
> A: To colors opal and opalescent. To notes C. and G.   845-1

> Q: What in me has such a strong relation to particular colors?
> A: . . . Egyptian influence . . . especially given to be servants— and services—in the temples of that period. These colors as we

find, are especially those that tend towards those of the opal . . .

2120-1

More on Opal

Opals have a bad reputation, which began with the publication in 1829 of Sir Walter Scott's book called *Anne of Geierstein*. Readers came to believe that a character was a victim of a cursed opal. In fact, Scott did not intend to represent the opal as unlucky.

In actuality, opals have had a stellar reputation through the ages. The ancient Greeks believed opals gave prophetic abilities to their owners, and in the East, opals were seen as the embodiment of the Spirit of Truth.

In reviewing the readings, the Source was also asked about this unfortunate reputation and confirmed that opals can help with your own anger or anger that is directed at you by other people.

Fire Opal

The fire opal is mentioned seven times in six documents.

The readings give a clear differentiation between regular opals and the fiery versions of the stone.

Today, the most common opals are the Australian variety, which appear in the typical traditional colors of pinks, blues, and greens. In Mexico, however, there are bright red, fiery opals that are quite remarkable.

Recently, a gorgeous piece of fire opal surrounded by a pale pink agate caught my eye. A friend noticed my fascination and bought it for me for my birthday. I regard it as one of my very favorite stones. As mentioned previously, my sun sign is Aries. Therefore, I imagine that the Source might not approve of my choice. Nevertheless, sometimes it is important to use your intuition. In this case, there was something about that piece that immediately resonated with me.

I believe that there are powerful energies in the area of what is now Mexico. Those areas were once Lemuria and Atlantis, and I believe many people who are drawn to the Cayce readings were incarnated there at one time or another. I feel that the fire opal captured my imagination because of those energies.

Let's look closer at some of the readings that refer to the fire opal.

In the first readings, Source acknowledges the idea of fire as a purification tool as well as the passion of fire and the ability of this stone
to awaken passion in the user:

> . . . fire opal would be of the stones that should be about the
> entity; for the holding of that fire, that vigor, that *understanding*
> that makes for purification, even though the fires of the flesh
> must be *burned out* that the glory of self may be made manifest
> in being a channel for the glory of the living truths to be known
> and experienced among others.   1193-1

> It will be found that the odors of henna, with tolu and myrrh,
> create an influence of ease, while the fire opal . . . brings great
> passion, intenseness, the abilities to lose emotions through the
> very center of the body for the closer association of the spiritual
> with the activate influences of mental self.   1580-1

The next person, who was born February 2, 1923, is Aquarius. Source
believes the fire opal would be helpful, perhaps to balance other elements in the chart:

> Hence the opal that is called the change . . . should be . . . about
> the body or entity oft. Wear the fire opal as a locket about the
> neck. This would be well. Not upon the hands nor upon the
> wrists, but about the neck.   1406-1

Next, Source describes how fire signs might fade the color from
opals:

> There being, then, individuals who when wearing a fire opal
> would be hard individuals to deal with when it came to sex . . .
> . . . those which indicate the fire signs in the aura of such
> should never wear opals, and they will even fade flowers when
> worn on their bodies. But the more delicate, as would bring the
> nature, is preferable.   5294-1

I find this idea interesting. In ancient times, people believed that opals could change colors, becoming brighter when success and fortune were about to happen and similarly fading out when something unlucky was pending. It seems that once again, the Source was tapping into some universal knowledge.

Another reading describes the passion of the fire opal:

> . . . as if looking at a fire opal—as a burst of enthusiasm, or burst of purpose, or individuality that would be indicated.
>
> 5746-1, Report #2

The following report is one of my personal favorites:

> My husband and I are owners and constant wearers of matched fire opal pendants about our necks.
>
> Only recently we were blessed to meet the owners of the 'Opal Queen' Fire-opal mine here in Virgin Valley in Nevada . . .
>
> From 3 P.M. until after 9 P.M. I handled hundreds of uncut gems worth a countless amount of money . . . after several hours (I was still holding one in my fingers), I suddenly was seized with a burning sensation in my solar plexus region. I became slightly nauseated—burned up—then chilled—and next completely weak and near fainting. Being a nurse, I excused myself . . . lowered my head to my knees . . . Shortly I returned to the opals—and the minute I began handling them once again, the same thing occurred, almost immediately . . . the owner of the mine, Ed Mitchell, told me he cannot view or handle precious opals for any period of time without the exact same thing happening to him . . .
>
> Now, can you shed any light on maybe *why* this takes place with opals (fire opals)? No other gems seem to affect us.
>
> 1193-1, Report #4

The member received a letter back from Robert O. Clapp, Director of A.R.E. Membership Services:

... opal was a control for anger and ... as a means of purification.
There doesn't seem to be anything in the readings to support
your reaction to opals ... What your experience does indicate is
that gem stones do have an effect upon the body ...

1193-1, Report #5

Mr. Clapp summarized this idea perfectly. Some of my students
have experienced harsh reactions to stones in the past. If that happens
to you, try to allow the stone to work through the energy fields until
the negative charge balances out. Your frequency will shift until the
energy transforms. Often when significant changes occur, they can be
frightening because they are so powerful. In the end, the energy shift
will be an improvement.

Yucatan Firestone

Yucatan firestone is mentioned three times in three documents.

In my last exploration of this topic in the *Edgar Cayce Guide to Gemstones*,
I discussed the ambiguity of the term firestone. In that book, I suggested
that this term might be synonymous with fire opal. The theory made
sense to me because those kinds of opals are prevalent in the American
Southwest and Mexico where Cayce traveled during his lifetime.

I have since revisited this theory. Now, I am more inclined to believe
firestones may indeed be another version of the Tuaoi stone of Atlantis.
If not exactly that same stone, perhaps the firestone somehow powered
the machines of destruction in Atlantis.

The following reading gives our best clue to the true identity of the
firestone and suggests this may have been a destructive force from
Atlantis, which when used improperly would have devastated humanity:

Q: Give an account of the electrical and mechanical knowledge
of the entity as Asal-Sine in Atlantis.
A: . . . About the firestone that was in the experience did the
activities of the entity then make those applications that dealt
with both the constructive and destructive forces in the period.   440-5

In the following reading, Source seems to use the term firestone synonymously with the word opal, which makes me believe that Source is describing the fire opal from the Yucatan region:

> Before that we find the entity was in the Persian land . . . dealing in the linens of Egypt . . . the opal, the firestone . . .   5294-1

My conclusion is that perhaps Source was describing two distinct things in these readings and just happened to use the term firestone when describing a destructive force in Atlantis as well as the fiery opals found in Mexico.

If you decide to work with opal, allow the stone to reveal itself to you over time. You will reap the benefits.

■ P E A R L ■

Found in: Australia, French Polynesia, Persian Gulf, Philippines
Named for: Pearl is derived from the French word *perle*, which was derived from the Latin word *perna* for "leg" (as of a bivalve).
Birthstone: June
Vedic astrology: Moon = pearl

• Bible •

No mention shall be made . . . of pearls . . . Job 28:18

Give not that which is holy unto the dogs, neither cast ye your pearls before swine, lest they trample them under their feet, and turn again and rend you. Matthew 7:6

Again, the kingdom of heaven is like unto a merchant man, seeking goodly pearls: who, when he had found one pearl of great price, went and sold all that he had, and bought it. Matthew 13:45-46

In like manner also, that women adorn themselves in modest apparel, with shamefacedness and sobriety; not with broided hair, or gold, or pearls, or costly array; 1 Timothy 2:9

And the woman was arrayed in purple and scarlet colour, and decked with gold and precious stones and pearls, having a golden cup in her hand full of abominations and filthiness of her fornication: Revelation 17:4

The merchandise of gold, and silver, and precious stones, and of pearls, and fine linen, and purple, and silk, and scarlet, and all thyine wood . . . Revelation 18:12

. . . Alas, alas, that great city, that was clothed in fine linen, and purple, and scarlet, and decked with gold, and precious stones, and pearls! Revelation 18:16

And the twelve gates were twelve pearls; every several gate was of one pearl: and the street of the city was pure gold, as it were transparent glass. Revelation 21:21

• Cayce Readings •

Pearls are mentioned 199 times in 137 documents.

The A.R.E. received feedback about the effectiveness of pearls:

> . . . (951) wore a pearl on a necklace for about two years after Mr. Cayce's reading told her to. She could not discern what it did for her, if anything . . . I was studying astrology at the time . . . The teacher said there was a good aspect from the planet Neptune which governed pearls, so we felt Mr. Cayce was correct . . .
>
> . . . As I recall, the 'vibration' of the pearl was to do something. Whatever it was, I guess it did it, for I have had fair health all these years. The pearl was not demagnetized—I just wore it as it was. I felt nothing and noticed nothing personally, but chemical forces within me did eat a sizable hole in the side of the pearl. I take it from that, that I absorbed some portion of it. Finally, the entire necklace became so worn I discontinued wearing it. (I also absorb gold).   951-4, Report #22

> I purchased an oriental pearl late in 1941, had it set in an old fraternity pin, and now wear it pinned in my shirt pocket. As suggested in the reading, it has become a symbol of beauty evolved by action and friction through continued experiences in its own realm of being, holding ever to an unchanging purpose or ideal.

. . . the effect of the pearl has shown its influence in the mental, physical, and spiritual expressions in my own life. The continuous mental awareness of the beauty of the pearl resulting through action and friction upon a central purpose stimulates my mind to hold and know a main purpose throughout my present incarnation . . .

. . . I miss the pearl if I do not wear it. However, this may be a mental reaction. Be that as it may, the pearl remains an omen of the eventual full realization of my purpose in this three-dimensional experience. I have made progress during the past five years and will continue to wear the pearl for the results already obtained as well as those yet to come.   2533-1, Report #4

Here is the text of this person's (#2533) reading:

Thus the entity should ever keep a pearl about the self or upon the person, not only for the material vibration but for the ideal expression. For it will be an omen—not only because of the vibrations that it may give to self but because of keeping the even temperament, yea the temper itself. For the entity can get mad, and when it is mad, it is really mad!

Thus the entity became an interpreter of signs . . . in that experience owned the larger collection of pearls from the Persian Gulf and area—which is still the source of the most beautiful of these precious stones.

Keep such an one about the body, not only because of the vibrations but because of the abilities indicated. For, as is realized—and is oft analyzed by the entity—this is among those of the precious stones that indicates in its formation, in its beauty, the hardships overcome by the very source that made the beauty of the stone itself.

Q: What hobbies will benefit me . . . ?

A: The study of stones—especially precious stones. Not necessarily owning of same, but what part they have played, do not play in the lives of the idle rich, nor of those so begone by carnal forces; rather as that ye may gain by keeping a pearl close about thy body.   2533-1

The previous reading suggests that pearls, like opals, are good for quelling anger. The Source also reveals one of the long-held beliefs about pearls as a symbol of purity and higher ideals.

In the next reading, Source describes why the pearl calms the mood simply because of the pressures associated with its creation:

> . . . pearls unusual in their effect upon the entity, especially in moods . . . as indicated in the pearl—which has been produced by irritations. Hence, the ability to build resistances is a natural influence that comes about same, and not as a talisman for preventing this or that—but that the vibrations created make for same.   1189-1

> Q: My Life Reading suggested the wearing of pearls next to my skin for the healing vibration. Does the pearl necklace I'm now wearing help or hinder?
> A: When its vibrations have taken the body-forces, it will be well. Or if the body would demagnetize the necklace as it is, it would be more helpful for the body. Do not touch with same, but expose necklace to the ultra-violet ray for one-tenth of a second, or as a flash. This will demagnetize it and set it for better body vibration for this body.   951-6

The concept of demagnetizing a stone is something I have thought about over the years, although not particularly in this same context.

In gem healing, any time you use a stone and place it on the body, you will immediately feel a rush of energy or a shift in your energy field. The change in energy happens as you achieve energetic rapport with the frequency of the stone. Similar to tuning a guitar, when you have a string out of tune, you make adjustments until the strings are in harmony. To do this, you hold the guitar, strum the string while hitting a key on a piano, for example, and make adjustments until the two sound the same. Healing works the same way. If there is discord in the body, simply adjust the frequency until it feels the same as harmony in the body.

When the Source describes demagnetization in the previous reading, I am inclined to believe this is another way to describe the process of attunement. If your energy field shifts and changes as a result of wearing or using gemstones, ultimately you will no longer feel a powerful alteration when your frequency has achieved a new reality. Therefore, a sense of non-effect takes hold, which you might consider to be demagnetization. The fact is that once you make the shift, you will no longer need to wear or use the stone.

This attunement happens all the time. Let's say, for example, that you bought a piece of jewelry. Perhaps you wore it non-stop for several years. Then some years later while rummaging through the jewelry box, you find that same, once-beloved ring. You had forgotten all about that piece of jewelry. At this time, you have no desire to wear that once-treasured possession even though you might still have fond memories of it.

Here are some readings about past lives featuring pearls:

> In the latter portion of the life there were the interests of the entity in the pearl industry, in the Arabian Gulf and Persian Gulf . . .
> 1561-1

> . . . pearls that came from the sea near what is now called Madagascar . . .   294-148

> Also there were in the experience those things that make for what is ordinarily termed or considered royalty . . . pearls . . . etc. . . .   630-2

> . . . For there again the entity became the keeper of exchanges for many lands . . . golds of Africa to the changes of the pearls . . .   1213-1

> Wear . . . the pearl . . . but never upon the neck or in the ears— rather upon the extremities; for they will make for the bringing out . . . of those very colors and vibrations that have been indicated to which the entity is so sensitive.   1406-1

And Cayce gave a reading for someone who lived in ancient Greece:

> . . . certain character of pearls . . . would be well to be about the entity, because the very vibrations of the sea as creative forces,

and as activities through which there is the physical evolution . . .
1604-1

. . . The abilities as a judge of cloth, furs, and values, are a part
of the entity's experience from that material sojourn; also its
interest in stones—especially pearls . . .   2916-1

Cayce described a life of someone who lived in the Holy Land in Rome:

There the entity used what might be called the orange shell
game—finding a pea under a shell, only the entity used as a pearl
taken from the Persian Gulf.   3663-1

Source describes the most beneficial vibrations in the following
reading:

Q: What precious stone sends out the most healing vibrations
for my body?
A: Those of the pearl . . .   275-31

Q: What metal and stones hold the better vibrations for me?
A: The pearl as the stone, zinc as the metal.   2746-1

Source interpreted a dream featuring pearls:

Q: Tuesday morning, June 11, I saw a string of pearls, the words,
'Why throw pearls?'
A: Pearls the emblematical condition of tears as has been seen by
the entity and the representation of sorrow in someone whom
the entity has contacted . . . 'Why throw pearls,' why give out
that will cause the condition to arise (it is of tears, see?) . . .
900-81

Finally, Source sums up the virtues of pearls in this reading:

. . . the seven virtues,—hence seven stones, in the varied colors
. . . the pearl . . . faith . . .   533-20

Pearl of Great Price

This pearl is mentioned eleven times in nine documents.

The Cayce readings also feature major sections, which are not all included here, about the "pearl of great price," in which Jesus compares the journey to heaven to a search for fine pearls.

Here is the reference from the King James Version of the Bible:

> Again, the kingdom of heaven is like unto a merchant man, seeking goodly pearls: Who, when he had found one pearl of great price, went and sold all that he had, and bought it. Matthew 13:45-46

And here are some of the various readings that feature this phrase:

> Hence from those experiences we find the pearls of great price ...
>
> For the entity learned that the pearls of great price are not merely those activities from the affliction of a mollusk in the sea as it resists; but that as ye in thy experience resist that as would lead to selfish desires, the gratifying or selfish motives, ye build the pearls of great price. 2560-1

> A pearl is an adornment, a thing of beauty, created through the irritation of that which manifests itself in a lowly way to those that consider themselves of high estate; but by the very act of irritation to its own vibration is the higher vibration created, or brings about the pearl of great price ...
>
> Through such irritation, though, oft does the soul grow, even as the pearl ... 254-68

> Q: Should I continue helping in the spiritual lives of others?
> A: As indicated ... ye may make in the experience of others that which will make each soul find the pearl of great price. 764-1

> ... listen at pearls of great price yet have no thought, no mind, no purpose for same. 2067-1

Pearls before Swine

This phrase is mentioned twenty–two times in twenty–one documents. The other concept in the readings that is mentioned many times is the reference to pearls before swine. Here it is again from the King James Version:

> Give not that which is holy unto the dogs, neither cast ye your pearls before swine, lest they trample them under their feet, and turn again and rend you. Matthew 7:6

This important lesson means that you should not give your valuable possessions or ideas to people who do not appreciate them.

Why waste the best of yourself on people who do not treasure your value? Most of us undervalue ourselves at times, and apparently Source felt this reiteration of self–love and self–value to be important enough for Cayce to mention often in the readings, including the following:

> Unless these are in accord, *do not* cast pearls before swine! (Matthew 7:6) This we see should be the rule, absolute, would the work, as it is contemplated and has been done, succeed . . .
> 254-15

> . . . there are in their experiences in the present *opportunities* for service! *Do not sow* thy pearls before swine . . .   254-96

> Learn ye then that lesson in the present, 'Cast not pearls before dogs nor swine.' . . .   2067-1

> Q: Should this message be sent . . . to help them?
> A: Cast not thine pearls before swine; neither make thine house of no estate. Pity is akin to love. Love him that hateth thee . . .
> 257-61

More on Pearls

Although we use pearls as gemstones, they are organic, being formed from living creatures.

Revisiting the Cayce readings for this project rejuvenated me and provided much intellectual stimulation for several areas of my life, as the readings always do for me. The idea that the pearl originates from an irritant and thus assists us with anger issues makes complete sense to me. Have you ever worked with homeopathy? The philosophy of that discipline is that in order to heal from an ailment, you must ingest it. It makes sense, therefore, to use a material that has irritation as its fundamental building block to rid us of irritations. Brilliant!

My prior understanding of working with pearls was capitalizing on their ability to impart innocence and purity to the wearer. They were perfect to use for a woman on her wedding day, for example.

If you remember the television show *Leave it to Beaver* back in the old days, the pearls on June Cleaver reminded me of someone who exemplified the perfect mother and wife. Thinking about that show and others like it brings a nostalgic feeling for the innocence of a time when life was simpler. Similarly, when you see someone wearing pearls, it can give you a warm and fuzzy feeling.

For whatever reason, if you need to appear innocent to others, pearl is the stone to choose. If you are meeting your potential in-laws for the first time; going on an important job interview; or undertaking a situation requiring you to appear morally steadfast, devoted, and innocent—wear the pearl!

Years ago on a trip to India, I had the opportunity to have my palms read one evening. The palmist approached me while I sat under a tarp on a dirt floor near a restaurant where my friends and I were about to have dinner. The palm reader walked to the table to see if anyone wanted a reading. I thought this sounded like a once-in-a-lifetime chance, so I agreed.

The reader told me that to attract love I should wear a pearl ring on the little finger of the left hand. He said that wearing a pearl strengthens the planet Venus and thus brings love into your life. I am passing that wisdom on to you now; try it, if love is what you seek!

If you study a chart of the palm, which is what the reader interprets, the marriage sector is located directly under the little finger on the palm. The heart can be accessed by working with the area under the ring finger, which is also appropriate since that is typically where we wear a wedding ring.

Pearls have had long associations with love. Strings of pearls covered the coffin of Mumtaz Mahal after her death. Of all stones, the pearl was appropriate because the Taj Mahal represented a pure form of divine love as well as the loving devotion that the grieving husband had for his deceased wife.

▪ PERIDOT, A.K.A. CHRYSOLITE OR OLIVINE ▪

Found in: Antarctica, Argentina, Australia, China, Czech Republic, Germany, France, Namibia, USA

Named for: *Péridot* is the French word for "olivine," and chrysolite is derived from the Greek words for "gold" and "stone."

Birthstone: August

• Bible •

> And the foundations of the wall of the city were garnished with all manner of precious stones . . . the seventh, chrysolite . . .
> Revelation 21:19-20

• Cayce Readings •

Chrysolite, which is another term for peridot, is mentioned four times in two documents.

The Romans believed that peridot, which is also called chrysolite, would protect a person from melancholy, as substantiated by the Source:

> As to stones . . . preferably the chrysolite . . . will bring as an attunement the quieting, and the entity will find that whenever there is a feeling of physical depression, physical reactions that are as dis-ease in the body, the colors in any of these natures or forms will bring quietness to the body; as in having about the body the chrysolite . . .
> Q: What is my seal?
> A: The shield as the center, raised, though, rather at the points than in the center, see? and upon same, the berry—as a snowberry—as chrysolite in color, and the purple as a portion of the outer part . . .   1626-1

. . . through its attunements, or through the visions and the associations of the entity; the chrysolite . . . For the color purple should be close to the body . . .   688-2

More on Chrysolite

I had a major breakthrough in my understanding of gems in the Bible while researching chrysolite. The Latin word *chrysolithus* means "chrysolite" or "topaz," and the Latin word *topazion* indicates a kind of chrysolite or green jasper.

I considered including chrysolite in the topaz section of this book, but refrained. After further research into the mineralogical term, I discovered the word refers to a high-grade form of olivine, which is a type of peridot.

More on Peridot

Loved by Cleopatra and prized by people around the world since ancient times, peridot is a stone that everyone should experience first-hand.

At one time, I acquired an entire tub of the volcanic material, including many tiny gem-quality crystals of peridot. These were wonderful specimens with which I continue to enjoy working.

I learned about the healing properties of peridot years some ago when a piece of it straightened my spine after a long car ride. Since that time, I have been using it successfully in energy healing with clients. I once placed a piece of peridot in the middle of a client's back. After the session, the client reported feeling much more aligned. The dull ache in her back had also disappeared.

Later on, I took many pieces of my peridot stones on a trip to the Seattle, WA area. The people in Seattle resonated with them, more so than in other areas that I have visited. I considered that perhaps their connection was due to the watery energy in the Seattle area as well the volcanic and fiery properties of peridot. I believed that the students were attracted to the grounding energy of the stones.

Reviewing the Cayce readings makes me wonder if peridot worked much in the same way as the Source said it would—to stave off depression. The cloudy weather in the Northwest has been known to engender a certain amount of melancholy in susceptible folks.

Several of my students in Seattle experienced past-life regressions, but there was no particular information to connect anyone to those stones. Although there was no concrete conclusion, I can report that everyone experienced feelings of peace and stability while working with peridot.

I call the peridot the "chiropractic stone" because I believe that the volcanic matter is like the spine of the Earth. When you align yourself with the Earth's spine, it brings you back into perfect balance. Whether you need physical or spiritual realignment, peridot is a powerful stone to use.

■ R U B Y ■

Found in: Burma (Myanmar), India, Sri Lanka, Thailand
Named for: Ruby is derived from the Latin word *ruber* for "red." It is the gemstone variety of the mineral corundum.
Birthstone: July
Vedic astrology: Sun = ruby
Chinese astrology: Tiger, dragon, dog = ruby

• Bible •

It is interesting to note that the word ruby often appears in the plural in the King James Version of the Bible.

. . . for the price of wisdom is above rubies. Job 28:18

She is more precious than rubies: and all the things thou canst desire are not to be compared unto her. Proverbs 3:15

For wisdom is better than rubies; and all the things that may be desired are not to be compared to it. Proverbs 8:11

There is gold, and a multitude of rubies: but the lips of knowledge are a precious jewel. Proverbs 20:15

Who can find a virtuous woman? for her price is far above rubies. Proverbs 31:10

Her Nazarites were purer than snow, they were whiter than milk, they were more ruddy in body than rubies . . . Lamentations 4:7

There are references to the word ruby in the singular in newer translations of the Bible.

And they mounted four rows of stones on it. The first row was a row of ruby, topaz, and emerald; Exodus 39:10 (New American Standard Bible, NAS)

You were in Eden, the garden of God; Every precious stone was your covering: The ruby, the topaz and the diamond . . . Ezekiel 28:13 (NAS)

the fifth onyx, the sixth ruby, the seventh chrysolite . . . Revelation 21:20 (New International Version)

• Cayce Readings •

Rubies are mentioned sixty-two times in forty-two documents.

> The ruby would make for the body that not as something which would be other than the power that self attributes to same, through its actual experience. But the light or reflection from same, worn on hand or body, will enable the body to concentrate in its mental application the greater—through the influences such a stone brings to material expression.
>
> In this particular one (the ruby) there is that fitness with that which has been the experience of *this* soul, this entity, through material expression. Hence it is an aid, a crutch to lean upon. But, as has always been given, let it be a stepping-stone; *not* that which thou *standest* only upon!   531-3

Mary Ann Woodard followed up with Mr. 531 about his reading and received this letter on 8/15/46:

> Do not remember how I came to be in possession of a small stone a few months after the reading, and far from being a genuine ruby . . . I admired the little stone while it hanged on my chain, holding an old watch which I had for over 35 years, and some way, somehow, watch, chain and 'ruby' disappeared . . . I do know that up to that time I had my ruby I was more

contented, and today I miss the contentment I had when I knew
I possessed the stone . . .
    . . . someday again—who knows—I'll have another 'ruby'.
                                                531-9, Report #11

. . . the stones of the ruby . . . though under stress it may come
into being; the valor and the strength that is imparted in the
inner influence of the ruby about the body.   1144-2

To what color, symbol or stone does the entity vibrate best?
A: The ruby . . . .and as to colors—the radiation of colors from
. . . the ruby . . .   2542-2

However, if the ruby is kept close to the body, it will bring
strength, power and might in a manner to the purposes set by
the entity, or those choices given.
    . . . the ruby; this should be worn by the entity always.
                                                2571-1

. . . the seven virtues,—hence seven stones, in the varied colors
. . . the ruby . . . indicating love . . .   533-20

The stones that should be about the body would be of the
ruby . . .   1222-1

Q: Ruby . . . ?
A: In the Roman experience we find the associations were most
helpful . . .   2322-2

The entity was . . . a carver of stones . . . as of rubies . . . and those
prepared for those in authority and in power.   3657-1

. . . Ye should find . . . the ruby close to your body oft, for their
vibrations will keep the vibrations of the body in better attune
with infinity and not with purely mental or material things in
life.   5322-1

More on Ruby

The red color in ruby comes from chromium, which is an element
that stimulates your metabolism and helps to burn unwanted calories.
The browns that deepen that red color come from iron found in hema-

tite and can assist you with circulation and temperature regulation.

In ancient times, the Burmese people wore ruby talismans to protect them against illness or misfortune. They called rubies with a good red color pigeon's blood, which the Burmese considered to be the blood drops of Mother Earth. Burmese rubies were among the gems used in the Taj Mahal.

People in the middle ages believed that rubies could predict the future based on the changing color of the ruby they wore.

Hindus treasure rubies for bringing courage, peace, energy, friendship, and romance to the wearer. They consider ruby to be the king of all precious stones, symbolic of a fire that burns for eternity.

A Beautiful Gift

Years ago I received a gorgeous, three-carat, pure ruby from India as a gift. At the time, I don't think I truly appreciated how rare it was. Stones that large that are not man-made are unique.

Rubies have captivated mankind throughout the ages. The jewel of love, the ruby carries the red ray, which is valued as extremely auspicious in many cultures. Red is a protective color, believed to ward off the evil eye. Ruby is consequently one of the most highly protective stones in the mineral kingdom. The healing potential of this carrier of the red ray is limitless.

In modern times, rubies have been used in laser technology. If you want to use them for that same purpose, allow your ruby to shoot with laser precision to any place on the body that is out of alignment. Notice how things are able to shift back to their proper place.

Like medical lasers, rubies cut through whatever is not needed on a spiritual level to bring out the true healing potential and perfection in one's spiritual body. Just as a sculptor takes a slab of stone and carves a masterpiece from it, the ruby cuts away at anything that is unneeded or unwanted, revealing the perfection of the true self. Ruby steps in to enable you to stand in all your glory, allowing the light within to shine its brightest. Ruby helps to attract love, aids with circulation and anything concerning the heart and blood, and improves the energy around you in general. Do you need to get things moving in order to attract new energies? Ruby will help to circulate unwanted energy away from you so that the higher new energy may easily flow into your awareness.

Grounding with the Red Ray

The red ray is the root chakra, which is all about how to remain grounded in the world. For years, I was a person who loved purple and enjoyed floating around in the ethers, tuning into the universe at large. Certainly there is nothing wrong with that proclivity. As time passed, however, I eventually bought a house, curtailed some of my traveling, and became more grounded.

Looking back, I attribute my change to a trip to Russia that I took in 2006. I knew I had been there before in a past life. When I returned to the United States, I bought a house, settled down, and began decorating my new place with gorgeous fabrics that reminded me of the beautiful trappings I'd seen in the Russian palaces. I even painted a few walls red, which represents the base chakra and complete grounding.

I will never forget the look on the salesperson's face in the paint store the day I went to choose the paint. He took one look at that cherry red color and said, "Are you *sure?*"

I enjoyed that color immensely and eventually accented the other walls in the room with a cocoa-brown color that reminded me of the Southwest. The place looked like a Native American kiva, which is a sacred underground chamber. When people visited, they always commented on how cozy and peaceful the energy felt.

Even if you are usually opposed to red, try it anyway. You might like it! As a color, I think that red has been appearing more often recently, concurrent with the need for greater grounding in the universal consciousness. With so much turmoil in the world at large, along with the fast pace of our society, our spirits crave a calm and stable environment. In healing, red is good for conditions of the blood, circulation, and heart.

Years ago when I began working on my PhD, one of the books that I read in one of my energy medicine courses was *Vibrational Medicine* by Richard Gerber. In the book, Dr. Gerber wrote extensively about the fact that he believes the ruby is, without a doubt, the most powerful healing stone ever! Using charts and graphs, he showed actual scientific evidence that depicted the vibrational frequency of the ruby. To this day, his research remains one of the most influential pieces of writing for me in terms of shaping how I think about energy medicine. If you haven't read this book yet, I highly encourage you to do so. Unfortunately, Dr. Gerber passed away several years ago, but he lives on through his influential and brilliant work.

Focused Attention

I talked to a friend of my grandmother's today. She is ninety-two years old and sharp as a tack. She has studied many metaphysical disciplines in her lifetime. In fact, she had a friend who knew Edgar Cayce personally.

We chatted about how many kids today are so glued to their mobile phones, electronic tablets, and text messaging that they are completely oblivious to the here and now.

Our obsession with machines is a widespread problem in society today. We are often scattered and too busy communicating electronically to think about or notice what is right in front of us, to drive our cars, or to listen to actual conversations with people in person.

I believe we are heading in a direction reminiscent of Atlantis. I sincerely hope that we will collectively turn things around and put our priorities in order.

I have always been a multitasker—I talk on the phone, send email, and do several projects all at once. I am trying to get better about multitasking as I "mature," but I am still distracted at times. Having the red color in my house has helped my productivity levels tremendously. It has definitely taught me something about being present.

During these more grounded years, I have enjoyed working with rubies more than ever before. The red-ray energy supports the intention of being. As the Source said, the ruby can impart feelings of mental toughness and strength, both physical and emotional, while sparking feelings of love on a universal and personal level.

At different phases of your life, you will have different levels of awareness. I am experiencing a wonderfully grounded phase right now, which is quite unlike previous years when I raced around the globe without a care in the world.

If you are someone who finds great peace by being grounded, staying home, and simply "being," the red ray facilitates this desire. Likewise, if you are scattered and in need of some grounding, try working with ruby and the color red.

Ruby will work wonders for you when it is time to settle yourself into any routine. Your soul will be attracted to it at an unconscious level, and then you will work with the red ray. That's what happened to me!

To use these stones in healing, you can either hold the ruby in your hand or better yet, place it or wear it over the heart to allow a powerful opening there. If you haven't experienced rubies before, I think you will find that they have delightful energy.

■ S A P P H I R E ■

Found in: Australia, Burma, Cambodia, China, East Africa, India, Nigeria, Sri Lanka, Thailand

Named for: The Greek word *sappheiros* means "blue stone" and "corundum" is derived from the Sanskrit word *kuruvinda*. Like the ruby, sapphire is also a gemstone variety of the mineral corundum.

Birthstone: September

Vedic astrology: Saturn = blue sapphire, Jupiter = yellow sapphire

Chinese astrology: Goat and rabbit = sapphire

• Bible •

> And they saw the God of Israel: and there was under his feet as it were a paved work of a sapphire stone, and as it were the body of heaven in his clearness. Exodus 24:10

> And the second row shall be . . . a sapphire . . . Exodus 28:18

> And the second row . . . a sapphire . . . Exodus 39:11

> The stones of it are the place of sapphires: and it hath dust of gold. Job 28:6

> It cannot be valued with the gold of Ophir . . . or the sapphire. Job 28:16

> . . . his belly is . . . overlaid with sapphires. Song of Solomon 5:14

O thou afflicted, tossed with tempest, and not comforted, behold, I will lay thy stones with fair colours, and lay thy foundations with sapphires. Isaiah 54:11

Her Nazarites were purer than snow, they were whiter than milk, they were more ruddy in body than rubies, their polishing was of sapphire. Lamentations 4:7

And above the firmament that was over their heads was the likeness of a throne, as the appearance of a sapphire stone: and upon the likeness of the throne was the likeness as the appearance of a man above upon it. Ezekiel 1:26

Then I looked, and, behold, in the firmament that was above the head of the cherubims there appeared over them as it were a sapphire stone, as the appearance of the likeness of a throne. Ezekiel 10:1

Thou hast been in Eden the garden of God; every precious stone was thy covering . . . the sapphire . . . Ezekiel 28:13

. . . the second, sapphire . . . Revelation 21:19

• Cayce Readings •

Sapphire is mentioned four times in four documents.

> Have always been interested in precious stones—am wearing a sapphire that means a great deal to me . . .
>   2533-1 (remarks after the reading by Mr. 2533)

> . . . Henry tried the rod on the . . . sapphire, but got . . .
>   3812-7, Report #26

Cayce received a letter from a Countess regarding a lost watch:

> I lost the watch 4 or 5 days ago in the vicinity, it is platinum . . . sapphires . . .

Cayce replied, telling her he would not be able to tell her about the lost watch:

Why? Because the forces or influences that would be contacted, interested in just such material things, would not be in keeping with the highest that may be reached in seeking things pertaining to the more spiritual side of life.

4341-2, Reports #11 and 12

More on Sapphire

Sapphire refers to any variety or corundum that is not red. Blue is the most beloved version of the stone, but it can also occur in what gemologists call fancy colors such as black, purple, violet, green, dark gray, yellow, orange, and white. The stones were not officially termed corundum until the 1800s, after a geological analysis.

I reviewed the New International Version of the Bible to determine the geological likelihood of whether or not sapphires occurred in significant abundance in the places where biblical history unfolded. Although the Bible mentions the term sapphire throughout, I agree with the other scholars who have studied these stones. Lapis lazuli was more likely to be the true identity of the stone called sapphire in the earlier King James Version of the Bible. The Latin word *sapphirus* means "blue gem." Throughout history, the region known as modern Afghanistan has been a major source of much of the lapis in the world today. Geologically speaking, it makes sense that the lapis material would be the sparkly blue stone mentioned in the Bible rather than actual sapphires, which are much rarer.

During his journey to Mount Sinai, God gave Moses two sapphire tablets containing the Ten Commandments. These tablets, made from the *Schethiyâ*—a sacred stone formed from the dew of Heaven—held the breath of God. The inscriptions that were drawn by fire on the reverse side appeared through the translucent stone.

Moses decided that the people were unworthy of the sapphire tablets and destroyed them, substituting them with tablets of plain stone.

Sapphires have been prominent throughout history. The Taj Mahal contained Himalayan sapphires. Greeks mined sapphire on the island of Naxos. The Persians considered sapphire to be sacred, believing that sapphires painted the sky blue.

In the Middle Ages, sapphire was used as a talisman to ward off illness, offer protection while traveling, and spare people from the evil eye or negative thoughts that were directed their way.

Buddhists believe that sapphires impart more peace than any other gem. They believe that sapphire stones inspire prayer and thus should only be worn by those who lead a pure life. The energy of sapphires can also be used to enhance circulation.

The blue hues come from iron and titanium. You may have seen beautiful multicolored crystals that have been painted with titanium metal. Sapphires have the titanium element within them, which makes the color so brilliant.

Have you ever wondered what creates the rough texture of emery boards? I hadn't considered that question until I learned that the coarse particles called emery, which is an abrasive mix of corundum, magnetite, and hematite, work perfectly for nail files.

Leuco Sapphire

Leuco sapphire varieties are optically transparent. All sapphires are among the hardest of minerals, and these are grown industrially and used in modern technology for such purposes as LED lighting, laser optics, and microchips.

Black Sapphire

Inexpensive black sapphires are protective in nature, sending a shield up around your energy field to protect you from any unwanted influences.

Padparadscha

One of the world's most expensive gems, this is a pinkish–orange-colored sapphire, which is colored from chromium, iron, and vanadium. *Padparadscha* is Sinhalese (the language of Sri Lanka) and is derived from the Sanskrit words *padma* for "lotus" and *ranga* for "color." This variety of sapphire will connect you to a form of divine feminine energy that will allow you to draw exactly what you want into your life without having to struggle. Receptive in nature, the stone will help you to be seen in a powerful light as a person of higher ideals.

Yellow Sapphire

Vedic astrology has played a significant role in my understanding of gemstones. Several years ago during my journey with Transcendental Meditation (TM), my TM instructor introduced me to some experts on Vedic knowledge. Shortly thereafter, I started having readings and learning more about the way gems are prescribed to people to aid with afflictions in the astrological chart. In Vedic wisdom, it is believed that the vibrations of individual stones work in alignment with the planets. Therefore, different gems can be used to strengthen planets that are weaker in a person's chart and help them to live a more balanced life.

I have had an interest in the yellow sapphires ever since a Vedic astrologer told me that the yellow variety would strengthen the planet Jupiter in my chart. I purchased a tiny yellow sapphire and have loved the energy, but to be truly effective, I needed to buy a large one of at least two carats.

I was told that citrine is a low-cost substitute for the yellow sapphire, and more often than not, I have used citrine with significant results. It is one of my favorite varieties of quartz that can impart abundance and high energy to its users.

Blue Sapphire

Ever since I saw Princess Diana wearing her blue sapphire engagement ring, the sapphire has captured my imagination. Apparently, many other people have felt the same way! Thanks to Princess Diana, sapphires have gained in popularity to be used as wedding rings for those who choose to be different.

Years ago after my Vedic reading, I discovered that the best stone for me was the yellow sapphire. As a second choice, my astrologer also recommended the blue variety because it strengthens Saturn. During my trip to India, I went to a stone cutting facility and purchased a blue sapphire. I love wearing it to this day. Do I believe this stone has helped me in specific ways? That is hard to say because I love to work with all of the stones mentioned in this book. Regardless of Vedic wisdom, I recognize that we often need different things at different times in our lives. I will use any stone or mineral that I am guided to use at the moment, regardless of what any astrologer or anyone else has told me to do. I believe our vibratory bodies need to be tuned up with any number of tools that have been left for us here by our creator. Stones, essential oils, certain foods, and vitamin supplements that, of course, contain various combinations of chemical elements, might all help us in various ways at different times. Our lives and bodies are in a constant state of change and flux. It is consequently important to become increasingly proficient in listening to your inner wisdom about what you need at any given moment. No amount of intuitive guidance from outside of yourself can ever supersede what you know to be your soul's truth.

Blue sapphires attune us with the blue ray that is aligned with the throat chakra. As such, blue sapphires will help you to tap into your hidden, inner wisdom. Sapphire allows you to communicate that knowledge through knowing what is best for yourself or for others. By enabling the throat center to open and your truth to come forth in a powerful way, you gain self-confidence and inner power. Speaking your truth, hearing your truth, and removing blockages to prevent that spiritual wisdom from shining through to you are all powerful benefits from working with this stone.

Blue sapphire will strengthen you. The more you are able to align with your highest self and your inner guru, the happier, healthier, and more balanced you will be. Your work will allow longevity and stamina to follow you throughout your life.

Sapphires are among my favorite stones of all time! I think they are some of the most powerful and healing stones on the planet because of the blue ray.

Blue Ray and Communication

The blue ray not only describes a high-definition video player in our modern homes, but for this discussion, it also refers to an important ray in the color spectrum that relates to the throat chakra center, which is all about communication.

If you are attracted to blue sapphire, ask yourself some questions. Are you speaking your truth? Are you saying what is on your mind?

And most important—are you comfortable with your truth even if it is politically incorrect or unpopular? Are you holding back your words to protect someone's feelings or because of your own fear?

Throat center issues are at the core of some of the biggest problems that are facing humanity today. Many New Age pundits say that our hearts need to be more open. I agree that is true, but the other often-overlooked area is the realm of the throat.

More and more we find that people are unable to speak their minds for one reason or another. When people pretend everything is okay, real improvement is not possible. Sometimes in order to make things better, people need a way to air their differences before they can achieve a higher understanding. In my opinion, we've lost evolutionary ground from our lack of honest communication. How are we going to have a dialogue about the bigger issues facing humanity if we have to walk on eggshells around each other? Keeping quiet to avoid conflict ultimately causes resentments and tensions to build that might eventually reach a breaking point. Breaking points are not good for anybody!

We need to be able to stand up and say what is on our minds. If you require assistance in this area, the blue sapphire will help you.

There are other sapphires that are not mentioned here that come in multiple colors. If and when you stumble upon one, the color of the stone you choose will affect how it works for your healing. Many will resonate with the same energies as the colors of the chakra centers. Because the sapphire in general is a superb transmitter and a tough stone, the colored sapphires will amplify energy and encourage things to move in the right direction.

I hope you will experiment with one of my favorite stones on earth. Enjoy!

■TOPAZ■

Found in: Afghanistan, Australia, Burma (Myanmar), China, Egypt, India, Indonesia, Mexico, Norway, Pakistan, Russia, South Africa, Sri Lanka, Texas, USA

Named for: Topaz is derived from the Greek word *Topázios*, referring to St. John's Island in the Red Sea, and may be related to the Sanskrit word *tapas* meaning "fire" or "heat."

Birthstone: November = yellow, December = blue
Chinese astrology: Rooster, horse = topaz

• Bible •

> Thou hast been in Eden the garden of God; every precious stone
> was thy covering . . . topaz . . . Ezekiel 28:13
>
> . . . the ninth, a topaz . . . Revelation 21:20

• Cayce Readings •

Topaz is mentioned five times in five documents.

> In this temple, we find these of large or semi-circular columns
> of . . . topaz . . .   364-12
>
> Q: Give exact location and depth beneath the surface.
> A: . . . in North and Easterly direction—topaz in quartz . . .
>   195-7
>
> . . . those colors that tend toward . . . the topaz, and in these—
> these; for the entity made same those of the scarabs that later
> became sacred to those peoples.   2120-1

Pliny called topaz the stone of strength, and in this reading, Source
recognizes that same energy:

> . . . keep the topaz as a stone about thee always. Its beauty, its
> purity, its clarity, may bring to thee strength. For this ye have
> found, and will find oft needed in thy dealings with thy prob-
> lems, and with thy fellow man.   2281-1

More on Topaz

In the section on peridot, I mentioned my surprise to discover that
the Latin word *chrysolithus* means "chrysolite" or "Topázios," and that
chrysolite is also called peridot. Further exploration uncovered the fact
that in ancient times, the chrysolite was referred to as topaz. Through
education about geology and chemical elements over the centuries, that

stone has come to be regarded as peridot.

Superstitious people who lived during the Middle Ages believed that wearing a topaz set in gold on the left arm or around the neck would help to dispel negativity. They even powdered the stone, believing that it helped their insomnia.

Blue Topaz

One of my all-time favorite rings contains a stunning piece of bright blue emerald-cut (rectangular) topaz. Known as one of the stones of Texas—where I live—I call it my "Texas topaz." The stone is huge, and because I have very long fingers, I like the way it looks on my hand. I wear the stone when I need to communicate effectively. Any blue stone will help with communication, but blue topaz is especially beneficial because the blue resonates with the throat center. The size of this stone, combined with the healing, beautiful blue color, makes my communication more powerful and precise when I wear that ring.

I've also used topaz as a rubbing stone to calm the nerves during stressful situations. Do you remember when people used to carry "worry" stones? Usually, these were pieces of rock with indentations carved into them. You would put the stone in the pocket and rub it throughout the day to gain energy or release tensions. I use my Texas topaz that same way by rubbing it throughout the day, particularly if I am busy giving readings at a show. It helps to focus my intentions and enables me to listen to my inner voice in order to deliver the message the person needs to hear at that moment.

Topaz occurs in a number of colors. It imparts the energy of playfulness or joy and resonates with the spring season of renewal and hope. If you need to reinvent yourself, topaz will transform you into a phoenix, rising from the ashes into your new form.

Smoky Topaz

Another ring that I've loved for many years is a gorgeous, oval, faceted piece of smoky topaz, which is brown. As are all of the earth-colored stones, smoky topaz is a deeply grounding stone.

In the same way that the blue topaz instills a sense of confidence, the smoky topaz inspires self–reliance in a stronger, more protective manner. It helps to increase physical stamina when facing physically demanding challenges or situations where others may try to seize control over you. It is indeed a stone of strength.

Selecting Your Topaz

Your stage of life or particular circumstances at any given time will determine the color and variety of topaz that you will use. All the topaz stones, regardless of color, will bring confidence and strength to you in your endeavors. Whatever you choose will be for your highest and best good.

■TURQUOISE■

Found in: Argentina, Australia, Belgium, Bolivia, Brazil, Chile, China, Egypt, Iran, Mexico, Peru, Turkestan, USA
Named for: Turquoise is derived from an Old French word for "Turkish," referring to the original Iranian material that arrived in Europe via Turkey.
Birthstone: December

• Bible •

The King James Version does not mention turquoise, but the New International Version does. I will include the stones mentioned in the NIV in their entirety so that you can see them all in context.

> the second row shall be turquoise, lapis lazuli and emerald; Exodus 28:18 (NIV)

> the second row was turquoise, lapis lazuli and emerald; Exodus 39:11 (NIV)

> With all my resources I have provided for the temple of my God—gold for the gold work, silver for the silver, bronze for the bronze, iron for the iron and wood for the wood, as well as onyx for the settings, turquoise, stones of various colors, and all kinds of fine stone and marble—all of these in large quantities. 1 Chronicles 29:2 (NIV)

Afflicted city, lashed by storms and not comforted, I will rebuild you with stones of turquoise, your foundations with lapis lazuli. Isaiah 54:11 (NIV)

Aram did business with you because of your many products; they exchanged turquoise, purple fabric, embroidered work, fine linen, coral and rubies for your merchandise. Ezekiel 27:16 (NIV)

You were in Eden, the garden of God; every precious stone adorned you: carnelian, chrysolite and emerald, topaz, onyx and jasper, lapis lazuli, turquoise and beryl. Your settings and mountings were made of gold; on the day you were created they were prepared. Ezekiel 28:13 (NIV)

the fifth onyx, the sixth ruby, the seventh chrysolite, the eighth beryl, the ninth topaz, the tenth turquoise . . . Revelation 21:20

• Cayce Readings •

Turquoise is mentioned eight times in eight documents.
One client wanted information about oil drilling possibilities:

> . . . on Arizona lands, for drilling oil, in which information was volunteered about . . . turquoise. In subsequent readings for Mr. (195) no mention was ever made of the Arizona Lost Sheep Mine.   195-1, Report #4

I did some research on this Lost Sheep Mine and discovered that it was located in the Superstition Mountains in Arizona, home to the Lost Dutchman Gold Mine. The Superstition Mountains were supposedly cursed so that no one could locate the riches thought to be buried there. Apparently the site of the treasure is known only to the Apaches, who have kept the location hidden since the 1500s to prevent outsiders from finding the treasure there. The area has captivated the imaginations of people throughout the world who search for this legendary treasure.

... minerals might be obtained ... turquoise. These could be
made to pay. These will be good lands.   195-5

Q: ... where does ... turquoise outcrop ...?
A: ... in the ridge that lies in the Western half of this Section ...
                                                          195-7

... influences that may bring the greater force around the body ...
in the turquoise blue ...   608-7

Q: What shade of blue should the entity use in her dress?
A: Turquoise!   694-2

More on Turquoise

Turquoise has been a treasured stone for cultures around the world
for millennia. Sacred to many Native American peoples, the Navajo
believed that turquoise fell from the sky, the Zuni believed it warded off
demons, and the Apaches believed that turquoise assisted in the hunt.

I grew up in New Mexico and had the opportunity to explore all of
the major mining areas as a child. One of the most interesting stories
is about the Cerrillos turquoise mine, located near the little town of
Madrid. The Cerrillos mining district was once a major source of gold,
silver, lead, and zinc, and Cerrillos turquoise was taken by the Spaniards
to be used for the crown jewels of Spain.

Today you can drive for miles on what is called the Turquoise Trail
National Scenic Byway, which runs on Highways 14 and 536 through
the Sandia, San Pedro, and Ortiz mountains between Albuquerque and
Santa Fe. Along the way, you can visit several old mining towns that
have been transformed into artist colonies and explore a variety of
interesting historic places.

In connection with New Mexico, one fascinating discussion about
turquoise in the Edgar Cayce readings involved the Mystery Rock in Los
Lunas, New Mexico. Some call it the Decalogue Stone, which is another
term for the Ten Commandments.

Commandment Rock, located thirty-five miles south of Albuquerque, contains an abridged version of the Ten Commandments in an
obscure form of Hebrew, which scholars say proves the existence of
ancient Hebrews in the early Americas.

While I had not heard of the Mystery Rock mentioned in the report for reading 5750-1 before doing this research, I can assure you that I'll be making a stop in Los Lunas the next time I visit friends and relatives nearby.

Undoubtedly, the New Mexico and Arizona region is geologically significant. The topography of this area is strikingly similar to that of the ancient Holy Land.

The Biblical references above do not substitute turquoise for lapis lazuli. The two stones do have a similar chemical composition, so I wanted to research the possibility.

Also, the King James Version cites emerald in place of turquoise. In several of the biblical passages listed above, the stone is not mentioned at all in the KJV. It is as though someone threw it in where it had not been originally. Debate over the true identity of these stones will continue.

Turquoise in Healing

Turquoise vibrates at a far higher frequency than many other stones and for that reason can be used in the center of the body to send out healing vibrations from the solar plexus throughout the entire being.

Turquoise helps physical situations by raising the frequency to such a high point that lower vibrational ailments will no longer be compatible. On a spiritual level, turquoise helps you to communicate and commune with the highest levels of spiritual wisdom.

Turquoise is highly sensitive to the temperature and oils on the body. Be sure to take off rings before washing your hands. Turquoise is a very delicate mineral, and the color can change or fade from too much sun, water, perspiration, cosmetics, or oil on the skin.

Many ancient peoples including the Aztecs, Mayans, Incans, Toltecs, Olmecs, and Spaniards wandered through the Southwest and Central and South Americas. The Cayce readings indicate that this area was part of the lost continent of Lemuria. Did Semitic tribes also wander this area, perhaps before the Mayan/Pre-Columbian influences settled in the region? We can only speculate.

All of these cultures worked with turquoise as well as with the minerals lapis, malachite, and azurite. These stones contain copper aluminum silicates and are not minerals found just anywhere in the world. They are special. The chemical composition provides an ideal conductive energy by which many people throughout history have connected to their individual understanding of the Creator.

Based on the influence turquoise has had on the people of the Americas to the indigenous peoples of Tibet, China, and India, the stone will not lose its popularity any time soon.

■ ZIRCON ■

Found in: Australia, Brazil, Burma, Cambodia, Canada, France, India, Russia, Sri Lanka, USA, and ubiquitous in the Earth's crust

Named for: Zircon is derived from the Persian word *zargun*, which means "golden-colored." It includes hyacinth, or yellow zircon, and jacinth, a transparent red variety of zircon.

Birthstone: December

• Bible •

Jacinth is mentioned one time in the King James Version of the Bible:

> And thus I saw the horses in the vision, and them that sat on them, having breastplates of fire, and of jacinth, and brimstone: and the heads of the horses were as the heads of lions; and out of their mouths issued fire and smoke and brimstone. Revelation 9:17

Jacinth is mentioned three times in the New International Version:

> . . . the third row shall be jacinth . . . Exodus 28:19
>
> . . . the third row was jacinth . . . Exodus 39:12
>
> . . . the eleventh jacinth . . . Revelation 21:20

• Cayce Readings •

Jacinth is not mentioned in the readings.

Hyacinth is mentioned two times in two documents.

One reading referenced Hyacinth as a street name; the other described hyacinth as a symbol. The symbolic reference probably relates to the term as it denotes the flower, a member of the lily family, which has ties to the Greek god Apollo:

> Q: Please give my seal . . .
> A: . . . On either side, at the top, would appear a *bell*; or the shape, as it were, of a bell from a hyacinth rather than a *bell* of a commercial thought or of such natures . . .   993-4

Zircon is mentioned one time in a letter written after Cayce's death:

> . . . whenever I saw a zircon with its bluish-greenish tints and I looked for the 'reddish' spectrum I was seeking that contrast which in reality gave the stone some life, regardless of the art of the lapidarist . . .   531-9, Report #11

More on Zircon

In the King James Version of the Bible, ligure is the stone named in place of the jacinth in Exodus. Modern geologists do not acknowledge the existence of any stone called ligure, but there is one called ligurite, which is a synonym for an extremely rare stone called titanite, containing the element titanium. Based on the rarity, I would imagine that a jacinth, which is a form of zircon, would be more likely to be a stone in the breastplate of the high priest.

These days you will find a large variety and many colors of zircons on the market, and they are priced based on the depth of their color. Many are from Asia.

The blue zircon is good for communication and helps primarily in the business sector rather than for interpersonal relationships. Blue zircon will give you eloquence in speech and allow your communication to be persuasive and effective, particularly if you are attempting to convince someone of your point of view. Zircon will benefit anyone in the communications professions and is also useful if you are in sales.

Red or brown varieties of zircon are called either jacinth or hyacinth. These colors can provide grounding, help prevent food poisoning, alleviate symptoms of food poisoning such as a stomachache, or assist with other digestive issues.

In general, zircon protects you and your belongings from accidents, bad storms, floods, or hail damage. By belongings, I mean your home and car. Placing a piece of zircon in the glove compartment of the car will prevent theft.

Prized in India, zircon is believed to bring success and material abundance, protect a person from poison, and create the energy of honor and wisdom.

If you need more material success in your life, especially related to your personal efforts in the business community, zircon is the gem for you.

PART
THREE

3 Stones of the Bible

In this section, we will explore some of the other aspects of the Bible and how stones played a significant role in those early times.

The Twelve Tribes

Edgar Cayce gave a reading in 1937 to the Glad Helpers, who were studying the last book of the Bible, Revelation.

> Q: Please explain the 12 names which represent the 12 tribes of the children of Israel.
> A: The same as the twelve gates, the twelve angels, the twelve ways, the twelve understandings; or the approach to Israel the seeker—all seeking not then as the expression of self but as one in the Holy One!!   281-37

Breastplate of the High Priest

There are several other aspects to explore concerning biblical stones, and one of the major points is the identity of the stones found in the breastplate of the high priest that is described in Exodus. For your reference, in this section I will list the tribes found in the King James Version of the Bible. In my book published in 2005 by the A.R.E. Press, *Edgar Cayce Guide to Gemstones*, I compared the various versions of the Bible as they relate to the stones, but I do not want to duplicate that information here.

The KJV mentions the twelve tribes several times, including the following passage:

> 1) Now these are the names of the children of Israel, which came into Egypt; every man and his household came with Jacob. 2) Reuben, Simeon, Levi, and Judah, 3) Issachar, Zebulun, and Benjamin, 4) Dan, and Naphtali, Gad, and Asher. 5) And all the souls that came out of the loins of Jacob were seventy souls: for Joseph was in Egypt already. 6) And Joseph died, and all his brethren, and all that generation. Exodus 1:1-6

According to the King James Version, (Exodus 28:17-20), here are the stones in the breastplate:

■ BREASTPLATE OF THE HIGH PRIEST, KJV ■

Row One	Row Two	Row Three	Row Four
Sardius	Emerald	Ligure	Beryl
Topaz	Sapphire	Agate	Onyx
Carbuncle	Diamond	Amethyst	Jasper

There are many differing theories—too many to count—about which stone represents which tribe. The previous list shows the tribes in the order presented in the King James Version, with the exception of Joseph. Normally, Joseph is second to last, represented by the stone onyx because the Bible states he was already in Egypt.

■ STONES AND TRIBES ■

TRIBE	STONE
Reuben	Sardius
Simeon	Topaz
Levi	Carbuncle
Judah	Emerald
Issachar	Sapphire
Zebulun	Diamond
Benjamin	Ligure
Dan	Agate
Naphtali	Amethyst
Gad	Beryl
Joseph	Onyx
Asher	Jasper

Studies from various spiritual organizations list variants of these stones, and several newer versions of the Bible offer different interpretations based on more recent knowledge about geology.

I have spent over a decade looking into this topic, and I can say that while trying to identify the stones has fascinated me, I am no closer to a definite conclusion about their true identities. Some things must remain a mystery.

■ CORNERSTONE ■

In biblical times, a cornerstone was used as a foundation for an entire structure. Once the cornerstone was in place, it provided the stability needed for the rest of the building. If left out or placed improperly, the entire foundation and structure would crumble. Once in place, the rest of the building would conform to the size, angle, and shape of the cornerstone.

Whereupon are the foundations thereof fastened? or who laid the corner stone thereof; Job 38:6

The stone which the builders refused is become the head stone of the corner. Psalm 118:22

. . . that our sons may be as plants grown up in their youth; that our daughters may be as corner stones, polished after the similitude of a palace: Psalm 144:12

Messianic prophecy describes the Messiah as a cornerstone:

Therefore thus saith the Lord God, Behold, I lay in Zion for a foundation a stone, a tried stone, a precious corner stone, a sure foundation: he that believeth shall not make haste. Isaiah 28:16

And they shall not take of thee a stone for a corner, nor a stone for foundations; but thou shalt be desolate for ever, saith the Lord. Jeremiah 51:26

The Lord of hosts shall defend them; and they shall devour, and subdue with sling stones; and they shall drink, and make a noise as through wine; and they shall be filled like bowls, and as the corners of the altar. Zechariah 9:15

Jesus saith unto them, Did ye never read in the scriptures, The stone which the builders rejected, the same is become the head of the corner: this is the Lord's doing, and it is marvellous [sic] in our eyes? Matthew 21:42

And have ye not read this scripture; The stone which the builders rejected is become the head of the corner: Mark 12:10

And he beheld them, and said, What is this then that is written, The stone which the builders rejected, the same is become the head of the corner? Luke 20:17

This is the stone which was set at nought of you builders, which is become the head of the corner. Acts 4:11

And are built upon the foundation of the apostles and prophets, Jesus Christ himself being the chief corner stone; Ephesians 2:20

The apostle Peter spoke of Jesus as a cornerstone:

Wherefore also it is contained in the scripture, Behold, I lay in
Sion a chief corner stone, elect, precious: and he that believeth
on him shall not be confounded. 1 Peter 2:6

Unto you therefore which believe he is precious: but unto them
which be disobedient, the stone which the builders disallowed,
the same is made the head of the corner, 1 Peter 2:7

The metaphor of constructing a house on a solid cornerstone to
tell the people about the importance of Jesus communicated the message in a way they could understand. The idea of a good foundation
is still powerful today as a symbol for the importance of Christ in the
church.

■BIBLICAL ROCKS■

Rocks, dens and caves, But I in none of these
Find place or refuge . . . *Paradise Lost*, IX. 6 118-119

Rock of Ages

The Bible mentions rocks as metaphors for the power of the Creator.
"Rock of Ages" is a legendary hymn about a limestone hill in an area
called Burrington Combe near North Somerset, England. The hymn's
author, Augustus Montague Toplady, wrote the following about the
miraculous protection he received from a sudden and terrible storm
while taking shelter in an outcropping of rock:

> Rock of Ages, cleft for me,
>
> Let me hide myself in Thee;
>
> Let the water and the blood,
>
> From Thy wounded side which flowed,
>
> Be of sin the double cure,
>
> Safe from wrath and make me pure
>
> Not the labor of my hands
>
> Can fulfill Thy law's demands;
>
> Could my zeal no respite know,

Could my tears forever flow,

All for sin could not atone;

Thou must save, and Thou alone.

Nothing in my hand I bring,

Simply to Thy cross I cling;

Naked, come to Thee for dress;

Helpless, look to Thee for grace;

Foul, I to the fountain fly;

Wash me, Savior, or I die.

While I draw this fleeting breath,

When mine eyes shall close in death,

When I rise to worlds unknown,

See Thee on Thy judgment throne,

Rock of Ages, cleft for me,

Let me hide myself in Thee.

(Lyrics from: http://library.timelesstruths.org/music/Rock_of_Ages/)

■ STONE OF DESTINY ■

And he lighted upon a certain place, and tarried there all night, because the sun was set; and he took of the stones of that place, and put them for his pillows, and lay down in that place to sleep. Genesis 28:11

And Jacob rose up early in the morning, and took the stone that he had put for his pillows, and set it up for a pillar, and poured oil upon the top of it. Genesis 28:18

In the book of Genesis, Jacob finds a stone in the desert and uses it to rest his head. The stone, currently known as the Stone of Destiny, Jacob's Pillow, or the Stone of Scone, revealed an amazing dream to him about a ladder reaching up to heaven. Jacob carried this stone with him and learned that the Stone of Destiny would witness the coronation of every ruler of God's people until the return of the Lord.

Nobody knew where this stone was until it turned up in Great Britain and was supposedly present even during the coronation of none other than Queen Elizabeth II. Also known as the Coronation Stone, it is a block of sandstone kept in an old abbey in Scone, Scotland.

Scottish legend says the Stone of Destiny originally belonged to Jacob. The stone served as the pillow where Jacob rested his head and had his dream about a ladder leading to heaven. The stone left the Holy Land and went to Egypt, Sicily, and Spain before it was taken to Ireland in the 700s and used for coronations there until the Scots stole it from them during a raid. The stone arrived in the village of Scone around 840.

For centuries, several Scottish monarchs used the Stone of Scone as part of their coronation ceremonies. In 1296, Edward I invaded Scotland and took the stone to London. Edward I built a special coronation chair to encase the stone, and placed it in Westminster Abbey as a symbol that the monarchy would rule both England and Scotland, but historians debate this "Westminster Stone's" authenticity as Jacob's Stone of Destiny.

After the crowning of James I of Scotland as monarch occurred on the Stone of Scone, some believed that the prophecy regarding Scottish rule had finally happened. The Scottish weren't finished with the stone yet. In 1950, Scottish nationalists stole the stone from Westminster Abbey. The British government recovered it but eventually gave in and officially returned the Stone of Scone to Scotland in 1996.

Of course, as with all things of this nature, some people believe the stone is a fraud and not at all associated with Jacob. Nevertheless, the stone is sacred to the Scots and Brits who have used it to crown their kings and queens and therefore must have some extraordinary power associated with it.

▪ WHITE STONE OF REVELATION ▪
• Bible •

> He that hath an ear, let him hear what the Spirit saith unto the churches; To him that overcometh will I give to eat of the hidden manna, and will give him a white stone, and in the stone a new name written, which no man knoweth saving he that receiveth it. Revelation 2:17

• Cayce Readings •

A white stone is mentioned eleven times in ten documents.

> My Life Reading told me that the crystal or any white stone
> carried on my body would be a helpful influence . . . I began car-
> rying a small, clear, hexagonal crystal of quartz, which, since it
> is a crystal and is descriptively 'white' or crystal, I have assumed
> is specifically what the reading prescribed.
>   This stone has given me a great deal of pleasure . . . it incites
> a pleasant nostalgia . . .   2285-1, Report #4

Source was asked to interpret the biblical passage from Revelation:

> Q: Please interpret the 2nd Chapter, 17th verse of Revelation.
> "To him that overcometh will I give to eat of the hidden manna,
> and will give him a white stone, and in the stone a new name
> written, which no man knoweth saving he that receiveth it."
> A: In giving the interpretation of this particular portion of the
> Revelation . . . the references—or all—refer to the physical body
> as the pattern, there is that as may be said to be the literal and
> the spiritual and the metaphysical interpretation of almost all
> portions of the Scripture, and especially of the Revelation as
> given by John.
>   . . . Each entity, each soul, is known,—in all the experiences
> through its activities—as a name to designate it from another.
> It is not only then a material convenience, but it implies—as
> has been given, unless it is for material gain—a definite period
> in the evolution of the experience of the entity in the material
> plane."   281-31

> . . . any white stone, has a helpful influence—if carried about the
> body . . .   2285-1

> In stones—the whiter, the more crystal the better.   1775-1

> As to stones, the blue or white stone should be as a lavaliere
> about the body. This is the better form of vibration for the en-
> tity, keeping a temperament gentler and more open.   2683-1

Based on these Life Readings, it would be easy to say that the white stone mentioned in Revelation in the Bible was a crystal, but I believe it was something else. Mentioned three times by name in Revelation, the white stone may be something other than crystal, perhaps something as sacred as the manna itself.

One thought is that in ancient times, the Romans used to award white stones with their names inscribed on them to the winners of athletic games. Perhaps Revelation's white stone was yet another ex-ample of the early church's attempt to speak to ordinary people in a language they could understand regarding the rewards that awaited them through Christ.

■ URIM AND THUMMIM ■

Urim and Thummim refer to the unique stones or stone tablets placed behind or attached to the breastplate that the high priests used to communicate with God. Urim is usually translated to mean "lights" and Thummim, derived from a Hebrew word meaning "innocence," is translated to mean "perfections." Urim and Thummim as "lights and perfections" or "revelation and truth" refer to the light and illumination that is experienced when there is a clear connection to the profound wisdom of God. The Bible has several references to this concept:

• Bible •

And thou shalt put in the breastplate of judgment the Urim and the Thummim; and they shall be upon Aaron's heart, when he goeth in before the Lord: and Aaron shall bear the judgment of the children of Israel upon his heart before the Lord continually. Exodus 28:30

And he put the breastplate upon him: also he put in the breast-plate the Urim and the Thummim. Leviticus 8:8

And of Levi he said, Let thy Thummim and thy Urim be with thy holy one, whom thou didst prove at Massah, and with whom thou didst strive at the waters of Meribah; Deuteronomy 33:8

In the following two passages, we see that Urim and Thummim are only to be used by a priest:

And the Tirshatha said unto them, that they should not eat of
the most holy things, till there stood up a priest with Urim and
with Thummim. Ezra 2:63

And the Tirshatha said unto them, that they should not eat of
the most holy things, till there stood up a priest with Urim and
Thummim. Nehemiah 7:65

There are some references to Urim only:

And he shall stand before Eleazar the priest, who shall ask coun-
sel for him after the judgment of Urim before the Lord: at his
word shall they go out, and at his word they shall come in, both
he, and all the children of Israel with him, even all the congrega-
tion. Numbers 27:21

To reinforce the fact that only priests could interpret messages, the
Urim withheld answers from King Saul:

And when Saul enquired of the Lord, the Lord answered him
not, neither by dreams, nor by Urim, nor by prophets. 1 Samuel
28:6

• Cayce Readings •

Urim is mentioned forty-six times in forty-two documents.
Thummim is mentioned thirty-seven times in thirty-three documents.
After the publication of the *Edgar Cayce Guide to Gemstones*, I contin-
ued my study of the Cayce material. I later discovered that Urim and
Thummim were featured prominently in the Cayce readings, and that
discovery was one of the reasons I felt inspired to write this book.
In a reading that Cayce gave for himself, he asked the Source to
clarify some things about psychic ability:

Q: What other glands in the body, if any, besides the Leydigan,
pineal, and glands of reproduction, are directly connected with
psychic ability?
A: . . . Hence these may be termed that the pineal and the Leydig

are the *seat* of the soul of an entity.

As to the activities of physical reproduction, much of the activity of the Leydig makes for that as of embryonic in its activity, or of sterility in its activity. So we have those channels. These are not the psychic forces, please understand! They are the *channels* through which the activities have their impulse! though the manifestations may be in sight, in sound, or in speech, in vision, in writing, in dreams, in Urim or Thummim, or in any. For these represent the Urim and Thummim in their essence, or in *any* of the *responding* forces in a body . . .   294-142

In the previous reading, the Source speaks of the Creator's communication through dreams or Urim and Thummim. The Bible states the same idea. Source reiterates that these are tools to access and receive higher levels of psychic or divine information.

In another reading, a woman asked Cayce how to communicate best with God:

Q: Is there any likelihood at the present time of developing a machine, based on the action of the electromagnetic cell, which may assist in securing direct communication as done by Aaron and Moses—and many others—with the Urim and Thummim?
A: Find in the self that as Hatshepsut put to self, in knowing who should be chosen—yet the trouble arose. Do not make the same mistake, that the vibration is the force—but that which impels same from the Creative Force. Such machines are claimed to be made. Some do, some do not create the right vibration. Too oft does there enter in those personalities of those seeking. Then, in self find the way to aid, and call again on Ra-Ta (294)—and on Hatshepsut—they are as Urim and Thummim, a channel only.
                                                                      355-1

In the last section, the Source seems to imply that Urim and Thummim are tools, just as Cayce himself (294) was a channel used to receive divine information.

The next reading further substantiates Cayce's use of the term by showing that information obtained from Urim and Thummim or dreams is more valuable than insights received in other ways:

> Q: Can the entity's psychic faculties be expressed or developed through numerology?
> A: . . . Hence *intuitive* force is the better, for in this there may come more the union of the spirit of truth with Creative Energy; thus the answers may be *shown* thee, whether in Urim, in Thummim, in dream, in numbers . . .   261-15

Cayce describes how tools such as Urim and Thummim should be used to gain clarity and direction in life. A woman asked for guidance during her reading and learned this would take place through a divine connection and acknowledgment of the Creator using Urim and Thummim:

> Q: Please explain and interpret the urge which I have to engage in some constructive activity, yet cannot quite grasp the proper method or direction or procedure?
> A: . . . As He has spoken through prophet, through sage, through Urim, through Thummim, through dream, through vision, since man has been in materiality or in matter, so may the spirit of truth still give expression to those that seek His face, and to find expression of same among their fellow man.   338-3

On August 23, 1925, Cayce consulted the Source for insight about his dreams, and the Source again described how Urim can assist with earthly lessons and knowledge:

> . . . Now we find the body and the body-mind, and the desire of knowledge, of enquiring of forces pertaining to elements of development, are separate condition, or should be considered as such (if we) would understand in a material manner the conditions as pertain to vision, dream, or Urim, that would be made beneficial to body's desiring, wishing, to know these lessons that might be, could be, would or should be, gained from such as dreams.   294-35

Another reading on April 12, 1934 described Cayce's dream about his deceased mother. Again the Source explained how a spiritual connection from beyond the grave could come through dreams, symbols, or the Urim and Thummim:

> Q: Please elucidate upon the experience I had last month in New Mexico when seeing and talking with my mother, in which she materialized a silver dollar.
> A: As has been given, either by vision, by prayer, by Urim, by Thummim, by dream, or in the material things, may the vision of those that are in the heart and mind of individuals given through the powers of those in the spirit plane to enter into association, communication, or activity with those that they seek to guide.   294-174

In another reading, the Source scolds a questioner for vanity:

> Q: Which elements in particular would be of the greatest value to observe their effects?
> A: Elements as related to that thou hast in hand, see? . . . Dost thou hope in thine self to find in two weeks or two months that it took two men, guided by the Father Himself, eighty years to find? (Moses—Aaron—Urim and Thummim?) . . .   440-16

A housewife learned that as a daughter of Levi in a past life, she had experienced a strong connection to the Urim and Thummim:

> The entity then was among the daughters of Levi, and those chosen to make the vestment of the priest. And to the entity, because of its own abilities, there was given the preparation of the settings of the breastplate and the putting of the stones theron, and the preparation of the Urim and Thummim for the interpretations of the movements that came upon the high priest in the holy of holies to be given to his people in or from the door of the tabernacle.   987-2

Another questioner had a disturbing dream about his mother:

> . . . I swung ma around and threw her face forward against the
> wall, hurting her face severely. Her face actually hurt or seemed
> to when she awakened . . .
> Well that each individual attempt to correlate those condi-
> tions as do appear in vision, or through Urim, and bring same
> to consciousness, that the physical conditions may be developed
> and strength may be gained individually, that will assist in giv-
> ing much to self's satisfaction (never self-gratification) to self's
> development, to self's abilities to be of service to many . . .
>   106-8

Cayce described the protective nature of Urim:

> . . . This is the presentation of that force that will guide, guard
> and protect, would the entity but keep in that way in which the
> forces may be manifest to the physical through Urim or through
> the visions . . .   900-79

According to Cayce, the divine can pierce through the veil between
our physical world and the next through Urim, dreams, or visions. We
can use the Creator's energy to manifest protection and guidance in
the physical plane.

Several readings refer to the connection between Urim and the
Higher Self or the subconscious mind:

> . . . in the mental forces, the subconscious in its development
> takes hold, as it were, on such subject matter, such data, as it is
> presented in the sleeping state, and through Urim . . .   900-90
> . . . yet the Voice through Urim, through Dream, through many,
> will give that information . . .   900-151

In another reading, Cayce described a priestly adornment worn by
a woman in her previous life:

> . . . The color of the robe was pearl-gray, as would be called now,

with selvage woven around the neck, as well as that upon the edge, as over the shoulder and to the bottom portion of same; no bells no pomegranates, but those which are woven in such a manner that into the selvage portion of the bottom was woven the Thummim and Urim. These were as the balance in which judgments were passed by the priest. But these were woven, not placed upon the top of same. Neither were there jewels set in same.   3175-3

More on Urim and Thummim

I've done years of research on the breastplate of the high priest and the identity of the Urim and Thummim in the Bible.

My interest ensued after I read the beautiful book *The Alchemist* by the Brazilian writer Paulo Coelho. In the story, a king befriends a shepherd boy and gives him Urim and Thummim to help him on his path. Having learned how important Urim and Thummim were to the Cayce Readings, I was especially fascinated to find the actual identity of these stones.

I believe the Urim and Thummim were a kind of divine communication tool used for direct communion with the Creator. The question remains, however, whether these were actual stones, tablets, or some other kind of material.

The idea of Urim and Thummim as stones is a prevalent concept in Mormonism. When Joseph Smith received a message from the Angel Moroni, he journeyed to find several gold plates that were buried in the hill named Cumorah in Ontario County, New York. Every year on September 22 from 1823 until 1827, Smith made a pilgrimage to that site. He finally dug up the plates revealing the word of God and took them away.

Smith called the special stones both Urim and Thummim and seer stones, and he used these tools to help transcribe the messages that were recorded on the gold plates to write the Book of Mormon. Witnesses described Smith placing the seer stones in a hat and gazing at them in order to receive their divine messages.

In contrast, rather than referring to physical objects, Cayce and the Source connected Urim and Thummim with superconscious knowing-

ness obtained in the dream state or through deep prayer and communication with the divine.

The Bible seems to suggest that the Urim and Thummim were actual material pieces. I believe they were more like the onyx Shoham
stones worn over the heart that offered the priest a window into the
other world where he could communicate with God. No one will ever
know precisely what kinds of gems or stones were used at that time
in history.

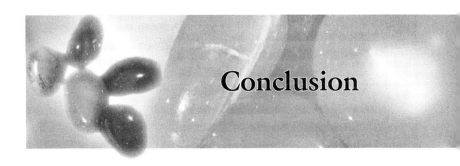

Conclusion

I cannot believe that ten years have passed since my first Edgar Cayce book was published. All these years, I have known that I was going to write another book for the A.R.E., and it turned out that the one I had been thinking about for years in the back of my mind was this one! It all started several years ago after a friend gave me a copy of *Gems and Stones Based on the Edgar Cayce Readings*, which was compiled in the sixties. That little book inspired me with the complexity of its material. I wanted to know more, and I still do! One can never finish exploring the depths of such rich material, but this is my attempt to give as much information as possible about the prior topics. While no research is truly ever finished, I hope that the research within these pages will endure. I also hope to encourage future scholars to pick up where others and I have left off to continue the study of Edgar Cayce's readings. I pray that the work will continue for many years to come because there is still much to learn from the wisdom that was imparted by the Source through Cayce's readings.

Studying the gem kingdom and learning how our ancestors used stones and gems are fascinating topics. I hope you will use the information found here to spark your curiosity and enhance your desire to discover which gems and stones you want to work with to enhance your life's journey.

During the frequency sickness mentioned earlier in the book, what I initially failed to recognize on a conscious level was the fact that on the day before my headache started, I had visited a friend who had just chosen hospice care. She was a huge fan of the Cayce readings and one of the many lovely souls I have had the privilege to meet and befriend during the many years that I have worked with this material.

I had had a feeling for over a month that something important was going to happen on January 15, 2015. I immediately decided to plan a trip, thinking it was what I needed to do, and when the plans fell through, I was disappointed. Nevertheless, an ever-present urge kept telling me that something significant was impending.

My friend had been diagnosed with stage four lung cancer a year ago, even though she had never smoked a day in her life. During the past year, we had spent many hours talking about how she might overcome this situation with her thoughts and by using the material we know to be helpful, including the Cayce readings.

While I was not able to see her as often as I would have liked, I did speak to her by phone. Each time, she sounded positive and hopeful, never willing to give up, and she was always a source of inspiration and courage.

Imagine my surprise to receive an email from her neighbor in early January telling me that my friend was not doing very well. I went to see her and at the time had not even realized it was January 15th until I had arrived at home that evening. That was the very day she chose hospice care.

"Are you scared?" I asked her.

"No. I knew it was coming."

Her next words surprised me.

"What will people think?"

Isn't it amazing how despite everything, good people often worry more about others than about themselves?

This brings up an issue that has always bothered me about most of us in the spiritual community. We believe that if we don't overcome every little circumstance with the power of positive thinking then there is something wrong with us.

I assured my friend that her journey had not been a failure. She had inspired many people along the way with her courage and wisdom—and especially me. None of us will get out of this life alive, and she had lived an amazing life. I told her that I believe in a life after this one and that we go on from here to a place far better. When it is her time, she is needed elsewhere, and her passing is meant to be.

As I was talking to her, I had a sense that I was not speaking these words myself. Part of me did not know whether these were appropriate things to say to someone who had just been given such shocking news about her imminent demise. She listened intently, nodded, and agreed. I soon realized that even though it was difficult to say, she had needed to hear my beliefs. I was probably the only person who was able to talk to her about them.

"Who cares what other people think?" I told her. "This is your journey, not theirs!"

And I want to say the same to you, dear friends. This is your journey. How you choose to use the information in this book is up to you. I honor your path and sincerely hope that this work may be of assistance to you in some small way.

Exactly two weeks after I had visited her on January 15th, my friend passed away. I had had every intention of going to see her again in the physical world, but I had been unable to go due to my own exhaustion during that time.

Shortly after hearing the news of her passing, my friend appeared to me in a dream. She carried a tiny box, handed it to me, and then floated away. I woke up and knew immediately that I would then fully recover. I used some Cayce remedies that helped greatly, along with the stones and a cleansing diet. The methods worked together to achieve a cure.

The moral of the story is to realize that there is no *one* magic cure for your life. Each step that you take and each remedy that you try is like a piece of a puzzle, and they all fit together. There is no right or wrong. All you can ask of yourself is to do your best.

Even more important is to spend more time seeing people rather than talking on the phone or emailing. Life is short. We need each other. I wish I had been there for my friend more often in the physical world. I am like everybody else—I do the best I can—but this situation truly reminded me of how precious life can be.

Finally, I am left with a feeling of how grateful I am for her and for all of the friends I have met through Edgar Cayce's work. Life is good!

Every time I embark on a book like this, I am continually surprised. I always learn new ideas and gain information along the way. I am left with the profound feeling that the more I research, the more questions remain.

This book has been on my mind for over a decade now. For years, I have wondered whether I would ever actually finish it. In that regard, I conclude with a feeling of gratitude and awe. Whenever I delve into the Cayce material, I find renewed inspiration for all aspects of my life. I cannot even begin to tell you how many projects, thoughts, and ideas sprang forth from the first book that I wrote, and I can't wait to see what will arise from this one.

Ancient mysteries will continue to inspire our imaginations for eons to come. I hope this exploration has provided a few seeds of thought for future generations of researchers. Above all, I wish you peace on your path through life. Enjoy the journey!

Bibliography

Ankerberg, John, and John Weldon. *What Do Mormons Really Believe?* Eugene, OR: Harvest House Publishers, 2002.

Auden, W.H. *Havamal: Words of the High One.* Princeton: Princeton University Press, 1930.

Balibar, Francoise. *The Science of Crystals.* New York: McGraw Hill, 1993.

Bauer, Max. *Precious Stones: A Popular Account of Their Characters, Occurrence, and Applications, with an Introduction to Their Determination for Mineralogists, Lapidaries, Jewelers, etc.* Rutland, VT: Charles E. Tuttle Company, 1969.

Berg, Yehuda. *The Power of Kabbalah: Technology of the Soul.* New York: Kabbalah Publishing, 2004.

Besserman, Perle. *The Shambhala Guide to Kabbalah and Jewish Mysticism.* Boston: Shambhala Publications, Inc., 1997.

Betts, Gavin. *Teach Yourself Latin.* London: Hodder Headline, 2000.

Bibles

21st Century Version.

American Standard Version.

Amplified Bible.

Authorized King James Version.

Common English Bible.

Complete Jewish Bible.

Contemporary English Version.

Darby Translation.

Douay-Rheims 1899 American Edition.

New International Version.

Book of Mormon, Salt Lake City, UT: Church of Jesus Christ of Latter-day Saints.

Brown, Brian. *The Wisdom of the Egyptians.* www.sacred-texts.com, 1923.

Budge, E.A. Wallis. *An Egyptian Hieroglyphic Dictionary—Volume One.* New York: Dover Publications, 1978.

――――. *The Egyptian Book of the Dead.* www.sacred-texts.com, 1895.

――――. *The Egyptian Heaven and Hell.* www.sacred-texts.com, 1905.

――――. *Legends of the Gods: The Egyptian Texts.* www.sacred-texts.com, 1912.

――――. *The Liturgy of Funerary Offerings.* www.sacred-texts.com, 1909.

Bullis, Douglas. *Crystals: The Science, Mysteries, and Lore.* New York: Crescent Books, 1990.

Bushman, Richard L. *Joseph Smith and the Beginnings of Mormonism.* Chicago: University of Illinois Press, 1984.

Campbell, Joseph. *The Masks of God: Occidental Mythology.* New York: Penguin Books, 1964.

Caradeau, Jean-Luc, and Cecile Donner. *The Dictionary of Superstitions.* Paris: International Book Promotion, 1984.

Carly, Ken. *Gems and Stones Based on the Edgar Cayce Readings.* Virginia Beach, VA: A.R.E. Press, 1993.

Cayce, Edgar. *The Official Edgar Cayce Readings.* Virginia Beach, VA: Edgar Cayce Foundation, 1971. (CD-ROM)

Charles, R.H. *The Book of Enoch the Prophet.* Boston: Weiser Books, 2003.

Coelho, Paulo. *The Alchemist.* San Francisco: Harper Collins, 1993.

Cooper, J.C. *An Illustrated Encyclopedia of Traditional Symbols.* New York: Thames and Hudson, 1978.

Cotterell, Arthur. *The Encyclopedia of Mythology.* London: Anness Publishing Limited, 1996.

Cotterell, Maurice. *The Tutankhamun Prophecies: The Sacred Secrets of the Maya, Egyptians, and Freemasons.* Rochester, VT: Bear and Company, 2001.

Crim, Keith, Roger A. Bullard, and Larry D. Shinn. *Abingdon Dictionary of*

Living Religions. Nashville: Parthenon Press, 1981.

Drury, Nevill. *Shamanism: An Introductory Guide to Living in Harmony with Nature.* Boston: Element Books, 2000.

Easton, M.G. *Easton's Bible Dictionary.* New York: Cosimo, 1897.

Gerber, Richard. *Vibrational Healing.* Santa Fe: Bear and Company, 1988.

Green, Miranda J. *Dictionary of Celtic Myth and Legend.* New York: Thames & Hudson, 1992.

Hackin, J. *Asiatic Mythology: A Detailed Description and Explanation of the Mythologies of All the Great Nations of Asia.* New York: Crescent Books, 1932.

Hafen, Leroy, and Ann W. Hafen. *Handcarts to Zion: The Story of a Unique Western Migration, 1856-1860.* Lincoln: The University of Nebraska Press, 1992.

Hall, Judy. *Napoleon's Oracle: The Ancient Book of Fate from Egypt's Valley of the Kings.* New York: Barnes & Noble Books, 2003.

Hamilton, Edith. *Mythology.* Boston: Little, Brown & Company, 1942.

Harlow, George. "Hard Rock: A Mineralogist Explores the Origins of Mesoamerican Jade." *Natural History* 8/91, 4–10. www.mesoamerica-foundation.org.

Hinckley, Gordon B. *Faith: The Essence of True Religion.* Salt Lake City: The Deseret Book Company, 1989.

Hulse, David Allen. *The Key of It All—Book One: The Eastern Mysteries.* St. Paul, MN: Llewellyn Publications, 1993.

———. *The Key of It All—Book Two: The Western Mysteries.* St. Paul, MN: Llewellyn Publications, 1994.

Jordan, Michael. *Dictionary of Gods and Goddesses, Second Edition.* New York: Facts on File, Inc., 2004.

Kunz, George Frederick. *The Curious Lore of Precious Stones.* New York: Dover Publications, 1913.

Lewis, Brenda Ralph. *Sutton Pocket Histories: The Aztecs.* Guernsey, Channel

Islands: Sutton Publishing, 1999.

Liddicoat, Richard T., Jr. *Handbook of Gem Identification*. Santa Monica: Gemological Institute of America, 1977.

Mac Annaidh, Seamas. *Irish History from Prehistoric Times to the Present Day*. Bath, UK: Parragon Publishing, 2002.

Mead, Frank S., and Samuel S. Hill. *Handbook of Denominations in the United States*. Nashville: Abingdon Press, 1985.

Mercer, Samuel A.B. *The Pyramid Texts*. www.sacred-texts.com, 1952.

Müller, Klaus E., and Ute Ritz–Müller. *Soul of Africa: Magical Rites and Traditions*. UK: Konemann UK Ltd., 1999.

Parfitt, Will. *The Elements of the Qabalah*. New York: Barnes & Noble Books, 1991.

Parrinder, Geoffrey. *World Religions from Ancient History to the Present*. New York: Hamlyn Publishing Group Limited, 1971.

Pennick, Nigel. *The Sacred World of the Celts: An Illustrated Guide to Celtic Spirituality and Mythology*. Newton Abbot, Devon: Godsfield Press, 1997.

Printz, Martin, George Harlow, and Joseph Peters, eds. *Simon and Schuster's Guide to Rocks and Minerals*. New York: Simon & Schuster, Inc., 1977.

Schumann, Walter. *Gemstones of the World*. New York: Sterling Publishing Company, 2000.

Seleem, Dr. Ramses. *Illustrated Egyptian Book of the Dead*. New York: Sterling Publishing, 2001.

Silverman, W.A., and Iain Chalmers (2002). "Casting and Drawing Lots: A Time Honored Way of Dealing With Uncertainty and for Ensuring Fairness." Oxford, UK: www.jameslindlibrary.org.

Smith, Joseph Fielding. *Essentials in Church History: A History of the Church from the Birth of Joseph Smith to the Present Time, with Introductory Chapters on the Antiquity of the Gospel and the "Falling Away."* Salt Lake City: The Deseret Book Company, 1972.

Tanakh: A New Translation of the Holy Scriptures According to Hebrew Text. The

Jewish Publication Society, ed. Jerusalem: JPS, 1985.

Ward, Fred. *Emeralds*. Bethesda: Gem Book Publishers, 1993.

——. *Rubies and Sapphires*. Bethesda: Gem Book Publishers, 1992.

Zim, Herbert S., and Paul R. Shaffer. *Rocks and Minerals: A Guide to Familiar Minerals, Gems, Ores, and Rocks*. New York: Simon & Schuster, Inc., 1957.

About the Author

Shelley Kaehr, PhD is a world traveler and an expert on energy medicine, ancient mysteries, and the healing properties of gems and minerals. Her work as a past-life regression therapist has been endorsed by leaders in the field of consciousness.

Visit her online at: www.pastlifelady.com

A.R.E. PRESS

Edgar Cayce (1877–1945) founded the non-profit Association for Research and Enlightenment (A.R.E.) in 1931, to explore spirituality, holistic health, intuition, dream interpretation, psychic development, reincarnation, and ancient mysteries—all subjects that frequently came up in the more than 14,000 documented psychic readings given by Cayce.

Edgar Cayce's A.R.E. provides individuals from all walks of life and a variety of religious backgrounds with tools for personal transformation and healing at all levels—body, mind, and spirit.

A.R.E. Press has been publishing since 1931 as well, with the mission of furthering the work of A.R.E. by publishing books, DVDs, and CDs to support the organization's goal of helping people to change their lives for the better physically, mentally, and spiritually.

In 2009, A.R.E. Press launched its second imprint, 4th Dimension Press. While A.R.E. Press features topics directly related to the work of Edgar Cayce and often includes excerpts from the Cayce readings, 4th Dimension Press allows us to take our publishing efforts further with like-minded and expansive explorations into the mysteries and spirituality of our existence without direct reference to Cayce specific content.

A.R.E. Press/4th Dimension Press
215 67th Street
Virginia Beach, VA 23451

Learn more at EdgarCayce.org. Visit ARECatalog.com to browse and purchase additional titles.

ARE PRESS.COM

EDGAR CAYCE'S A.R.E.

Who Was Edgar Cayce?
Twentieth Century Psychic and Medical Clairvoyant

Edgar Cayce (pronounced Kay-Cee, 1877-1945) has been called the "sleeping prophet," the "father of holistic medicine," and the most-documented psychic of the 20th century. For more than 40 years of his adult life, Cayce gave psychic "readings" to thousands of seekers while in an unconscious state, diagnosing illnesses and revealing lives lived in the past and prophecies yet to come. But who, exactly, was Edgar Cayce?

Cayce was born on a farm in Hopkinsville, Kentucky, in 1877, and his psychic abilities began to appear as early as his childhood. He was able to see and talk to his late grandfather's spirit, and often played with "imaginary friends" whom he said were spirits on the other side. He also displayed an uncanny ability to memorize the pages of a book simply by sleeping on it. These gifts labeled the young Cayce as strange, but all Cayce really wanted was to help others, especially children.

Later in life, Cayce would find that he had the ability to put himself into a sleep-like state by lying down on a couch, closing his eyes, and folding his hands over his stomach. In this state of relaxation and meditation, he was able to place his mind in contact with all time and space—the universal consciousness, also known as the super-conscious mind. From there, he could respond to questions as broad as, "What are the secrets of the universe?" and "What is my purpose in life?" to as specific as, "What can I do to help my arthritis?" and "How were the pyramids of Egypt built?" His responses to these questions came to be called "readings," and their insights offer practical help and advice to individuals even today.

The majority of Edgar Cayce's readings deal with holistic health and the treatment of illness. Yet, although best known for this material, the sleeping Cayce did not seem to be limited to concerns about the physical body. In fact, in their entirety, the readings discuss an astonishing 10,000 different topics. This vast array of subject matter can be narrowed down into a smaller group of topics that, when compiled together, deal with the following five categories: (1) Health-Related Information; (2) Philosophy and Reincarnation; (3) Dreams and Dream Interpretation; (4) ESP and Psychic Phenomena; and (5) Spiritual Growth, Meditation, and Prayer.

Learn more at EdgarCayce.org.

What Is A.R.E.?

Edgar Cayce founded the non-profit Association for Research and Enlightenment, Inc. (A.R.E.®) in 1931, to explore spirituality, holistic health, intuition, dream interpretation, psychic development, reincarnation, and ancient mysteries—all subjects that frequently came up in the more than 14,000 documented psychic readings given by Cayce.

The Mission of the A.R.E. is to help people transform their lives for the better, through research, education, and application of core concepts found in the Edgar Cayce readings and kindred materials that seek to manifest the love of God and all people and promote the purposefulness of life, the oneness of God, the spiritual nature of humankind, and the connection of body, mind, and spirit.

With an international headquarters in Virginia Beach, Va., regional representatives throughout the U.S., Edgar Cayce Centers in more than thirty countries, and individual members in more than seventy countries, the A.R.E. community is a global network of individuals.

A.R.E. conferences, international tours, camps for children and adults, regional activities, and study groups allow like-minded people to gather for educational and fellowship opportunities worldwide.

A.R.E. offers membership benefits and services that include a quarterly body-mind-spirit member magazine, *Venture Inward,* a member newsletter covering the major topics of the readings, and access to the entire set of readings in an exclusive online database.

Learn more at EdgarCayce.org.Learn more at EdgarCayce.org.

EDGARCAYCE.ORG